CYCLES

& Spirituality

Charting the natural signs
God gave each teen girl & young woman
to understand her unique cycles

Disclaimer

This book contains information pertaining to women's health. It is written for teenage girls and young women as a general reference and guide to understanding their menstrual cycles.

This book is designed to provide helpful information. It is not intended, nor should it be used, to replace medical advice. Readers with health concerns should seek the care of a licensed health care professional for diagnosis and treatment. All readers should consult with a doctor or seek medical advice before making changes to their diet and/or exercise plan or before beginning taking or discontinuing taking any medications and/or vitamin supplements. The author and publisher are not responsible for any specific health or allergy needs that may require medical supervision and are not liable for any physical, psychological, emotional, financial, or commercial damages or negative consequences from any treatment, action, or application of the information in this book. No medical or legal liability is assumed for adverse effects from following the information contained in this book.

Although every precaution has been taken to ensure the accuracy of the information in this book, the author and publisher assume no responsibility for any errors or omissions of information. References are provided for informational purposes only and do not constitute endorsement of any websites or other sources. Readers should be aware that the websites listed in this book may change.

All Bible verses quoted in this book are from the New American Bible, Revised Edition.

Personal stories in this book are taken from the author's own experience and from personal interviews with family and friends. Names have been changed to honor privacy.

CYCLES

& Spirituality

Charting the natural signs
God gave each teen girl & young woman
to understand her unique cycles

Alison Protz

Cover photograph, cover design, author photograph, and interior graphics © by Christopher Protz
Publisher: 380nm Publishing, LLC

ISBN-13: 978-0692542156
ISBN-10: 0692542159

Printed in the United States of America

To my daughters:
Haley, Hana, & Natalie

Acknowledgements

When I first learned to chart my own cycles, I immediately knew this information needed to be provided to teenage girls and young women. But it took a little longer to realize I was being called to the task. I am thankful to God for persistently calling and for the friends and family who encouraged and motivated me to pursue the opportunity to try to help others.

Thank you to my husband, Chris, for being amazingly supportive and helping me achieve this goal. Thank you for encouraging me to reduce my full-time job to part-time hours to allow me time to write. Thank you for your reviews, feedback, technical support, and advice so this book can connect with the greatest number of girls who need this information.

Thank you to my children on earth, Haley, Hana, Natalie, and Andrew, and to the children I never got to hold. Each one of you helps me realize part of God's purpose for my life, makes me strive to be a better person, and helps me grow closer to God.

Finally, thank you to the people who enthusiastically encouraged me to pursue this effort including Vivian Stooke, Kimberly Coltey, David Birchmeier, Stephanie Frazier, Michael Alldredge, Scotty Sparks, Sarah Howse, and the student couples Chris & I have taught through the Couple to Couple League.

Table of Contents

Introduction

Are your cycles perfectly predictable at exactly 28 days each and every month? If not, this book was written especially for you! If you have ever had a period that arrived "early" and caught you off-guard or if you have ever had a period that arrived "late" and left you guessing which day (or week) to be ready or if your cycles are so variable you can't even begin to speculate which weekend is more convenient for a camping trip, you might be amazed by your new ability to predict even the most irregular of cycles. If your cycles are already perfectly predictable each month, you may still find it fascinating to be more aware of your body and to discover how this awareness can improve your physical and emotional health and perhaps even help you develop a closer connection with God.

Cycles & Spirituality is about how cycle awareness through charting can lead to healthier cycles physically, emotionally, and even spiritually. *Cycles & Spirituality* can help you learn to recognize the subtle signs God gave you to understand your own body, predict your periods (even if they are very irregular), acknowledge your emotions, and manage cycle-related symptoms in natural ways. You may even be surprised when cycle awareness leads to appreciation: an appreciation of God's natural design for your body and for all things.

This book is not about puberty or all the changes that take place in a typical girl's body. There are plenty of books on that (see Appendix A for a good suggestion). *Cycles & Spirituality* focuses on your menstrual cycle – the entire cycle, not just your period – and how it is unique to **you**. Have you ever noticed a white, yellow, or clear fluid in your underwear? If you've ever asked about it, you may have been told "it's just discharge" or "it's normal". Well, yes, this mucus your cervix produces is normal but "normal" doesn't do justice to the amazing insight your cervical mucus can reveal about your cycle. Have you ever noticed your body temperature feeling slightly colder at certain times during the month? It may not have been due to the weather but to your hormones. **God's design for the female body gives us these creative clues that are unique to each girl on any given day of her unique cycle.**

Simply observing your cervical mucus and measuring your waking body temperature each day can help you understand when your body is preparing to ovulate each cycle and when to expect your period. It can also help explain other symptoms such as those occasional cramps that make you think your period is coming when it is actually weeks away or that random crying spell triggered by something seemingly insignificant. Before you panic at how strange it will be to observe these signs, rest assured that measuring your temperature only requires placing the thermometer under your tongue and observing your cervical mucus only means noticing the natural fluid (outside of your body) you probably already see each time you go to the bathroom. *Cycles & Spirituality* gives you the knowledge to understand the signs your body displays every day and to use them to predict your *own* cycle, however short, long, or variable it may be.

Cycles & Spirituality teaches awareness of what your own body is doing every day of your cycle, not just the few days you are bleeding.   Women who have this insight often comment that cycle awareness leads to overall better health. Being in tune with your own body's natural signs can encourage healthier eating, sleeping, and exercising habits and can help manage cycle-related symptoms more naturally, leading to improved physical health. For girls with irregular cycles, being able to predict the arrival of a period can reduce anxiety and increase confidence, leading to improved emotional health. Understanding how your hormones may be fluctuating on any particular day can also help identify when emotional reactions may be cycle-related. Believe it or not, the personal stories of many women show that cycle awareness can also lead to appreciation for God's design of your natural cycle, which can even lead to a spiritual closeness with God.

Cycles & Spirituality is written for unmarried young women who are not sexually active. It does not teach a method of preventing pregnancy. It teaches an understanding of menstrual cycles and how to predict them while keeping in perspective God's plan for young women. As this book is designed for girls practicing God's plan of abstinence before marriage, not all girls will find this book valuable. But studies show that more than 55% of teenage girls have never had sex and the most common reason given by them is that it is against their religious beliefs or morals [1]. For unmarried girls that have already had sex, reading *Cycles & Spirituality* with an open heart may guide you to God's grace and reveal His desire for your future. This book is prayerfully devoted to the many young women and teens who value chastity: may understanding your cycle while honoring your values have a positive impact in your life.

The first section of *Cycles & Spirituality* provides the background for understanding your female body in the light of God's plan. The second section explains the natural signs your body reveals every day and how to interpret them to predict when your period will arrive. Once you are equipped with an understanding of your own body's cycle signs, the third section of *Cycles & Spirituality* provides tools and suggestions for living naturally with the body God gave you. Being in tune with your body can reveal how some factors like stress, body weight, and medications can impact your cycles. The third section also acknowledges the many premenstrual and menstrual symptoms and provides practical and natural ways to handle them. From cramps and bloating to moodiness and stress, these suggestions are not the nonspecific "take an ibuprofen" and are more than "get some exercise". These recommendations take a natural approach and are based on medical studies and tried-and-true experience. They help inspire confidence in taking care of your body the way God designed it to work.

If you have irregular cycles, heavy bleeding, or difficulty dealing with premenstrual symptoms and have discussed any of these concerns with your doctor, you have likely been offered hormonal birth control (i.e. "the Pill") as medical treatment. The last chapter of *Cycles & Spirituality* discusses how the oral contraceptive pill functions and how it impacts a woman's cycle. This chapter discusses the benefits of understanding your natural cycles and investigating the underlying causes of cycle issues with the goal of empowering you to make an even more informed decision about the treatments you apply to your body. While the Pill has been shown to affect some symptoms, it is not without side effects, including the unfortunate side effect of masking the signs God gave you to understand your body and your health.

The intent of *Cycles & Spirituality* is for you many unmarried, chaste young women and teens to gain an understanding of God's design for your body. It provides the knowledge and tools to chart your own unique cycles, decipher your signs, deal with symptoms, and have healthy and natural cycles.

Note to Mothers & Fathers

As many parents have experienced or been forewarned, puberty and the years that follow can be a difficult time for teenage girls as they must learn to live with their changing hormones and changing physiology. Support from mothers, and even fathers, can provide great encouragement to daughters! For Christian families, it may help girls to hear reassurance that becoming a woman is God's natural design. But that thought alone may not seem tangible enough to help her get through the day-to-day challenges.

In His infinite wisdom, God gave each girl unique signs to indicate how her hormones are changing every day. Observing these clues can help each girl understand when her period will arrive (even if her cycles are irregular), how hormones may be affecting her emotions, and how to manage symptoms. *Cycles & Spirituality* presents this information in a manner suitable for Christian teenage girls and young women.

Cycles & Spirituality is not a book on puberty. It does not provide an overview of all the typical changes a girl goes through to become a woman. In fact, the information in this book may be totally new to you as parents. Sure, girls have been getting their periods since the beginning of time and the mechanisms of a girl's cycle haven't changed. But our understanding of those cycles, based on each girl's unique cycle signs, has evolved. Throughout the past century, scientists and medical experts in fertility awareness have come to understand that a woman's physical cycle signs (particularly temperature and cervical mucus) are correlated with when she ovulates and when she menstruates. This goes beyond circling the start date of her period on a calendar and counting the number of days until the start of her next period. Observing and charting a girl's unique signs with *Cycles & Spirituality* can give her insight into what is happening inside her body, physically and emotionally, on any day of her cycle.

Many Christian women who have learned to chart their natural cycles have commented that an awareness of what is happening physically and emotionally actually helps give them an appreciation for their bodies and brings them closer to God spiritually. For Christian parents, raising a daughter with morals and virtues is important. The teenage and young adult years are a time to instill and reemphasize values such as purity, loving as God loves, and sexual abstinence before marriage. While many secular media sources seem to strive against you as parents in these areas, *Cycles & Spirituality* can augment your efforts.

If the information in *Cycles & Spirituality* is new to you, be reassured that charting a woman's cycles is not an experimental technique, and your daughter is not exploring "uncharted" territory. Charting a woman's cycle signs is a well-published topic for use in Natural Family Planning (NFP) methods. In this context, married couples are provided specific rules for determining fertile and infertile times of the woman's cycle to either prayerfully postpone or achieve pregnancy. For unmarried teenage girls and young women practicing sexual abstinence before marriage these specific rules to determine times of fertility are unnecessary. But the benefits of charting and what it can reveal about a girl's cycles surpass fertility awareness when applied appropriately for each girl to understand her own body.

Cycles & Spirituality presents information girls deserve to know about their bodies in a context compatible with and supportive of Christian virtues.

Cycles & Spirituality is designed for teenage and young adult women ages 14-29. This book is not intended for "tweens" or as a first introduction to puberty for girls. The information in this book can best be utilized by girls and young women who have had their period for a year or more and are gaining maturity and interest in taking care of their bodies. If you, as parents, do not currently chart your own natural cycles, you can also take the opportunity to read *Cycles & Spirituality* together with your daughter. Even fathers can be encouraging by offering comforting words during emotional turmoil (the topic of female changes doesn't have to be a secret between mother and daughter!). As Christian parents, you can be supportive of your daughter's initiative to understand and take care of her own body in a healthy way.

Part I:
My Body, by God's Design

If you're excited about *Cycles & Spirituality*, you may be eager to learn how to get started with charting your cycles. Teaching teenage girls and young women how to chart their cycles, predict when their period will arrive, and live naturally with the cycles God gave them is the main motivation for this book. But simply learning the mechanics of charting your cycles wouldn't be complete if taken out of context of God's beautiful design for women. This doesn't just mean how 'amazing' a diagram of the uterus can be (feel free to insert your eye roll); it includes God's desire for women to love and be loved, to respect and be respected. In Part I, Chapter 1 discusses the benefits of understanding your own unique cycle for your physical, emotional, and spiritual health. Chapter 2 provides a background for understanding your body and cycles by considering God's great design for woman, for love, and for chastity. And, yes, Chapter 3 has a few anatomy diagrams and descriptions of hormones to help explain how your body generates observable signs each day – the signs you will learn to chart in Part II.

"For I know well the plans I have in mind for you, says the Lord, plans for your welfare, not for woe! plans to give you a future full of hope."

Jeremiah 29:11

Chapter 1:
Benefits of Understanding My Cycle

Charting your cycles means observing and making notes about your body's natural signs each day to help you understand your own unique menstrual cycles, even if they are irregular. God gave each girl subtle clues that reveal so much! Just by measuring your waking body temperature and paying attention to your cervical mucus you can decipher where you are in your cycle, accurately predict your period, recognize how your hormones may be affecting your emotions, and learn how to manage symptoms. Is any of that really worth learning about something as bizarre as *cervical mucus*? Many girls (including me) have found that cycle awareness through charting can lead to better physical, emotional, and even spiritual well-being. Skeptical? Are you thinking "How will I be healthier and closer to God by measuring my temperature and observing my cervical mucus?" When I first began charting my cycles, my only motivation was to determine when my irregular period would arrive, and I had no intentions of realizing any other benefit. But God works in amazing ways and cycle awareness soon led to cycle appreciation. Then, an appreciation for God's design began to extend to other aspects of life. You never know how God will work in your life.

Physically Healthier Cycles

Charting the signs of your cycle can provide great insight into your female reproductive health and overall physical health. Cycle awareness through charting can encourage healthier eating, sleeping, and exercising habits to aid in shorter and lighter periods (and who doesn't want that?!). Being cycle aware helps encourage a healthy body weight (neither overweight nor underweight) by showing girls the effects of body fat (both good and bad) on their cycles. Girls who chart their cycles can more easily identify potential health concerns or medical problems and take action to correct them. Girls who are aware of their cycles can use more natural methods to manage symptoms and reduce or avoid the use of over-the-counter medications.

And girls who realize all or any of the above benefits of cycle awareness may find these natural explanations and approaches to managing symptoms will eliminate their need to take "the Pill". Avoiding the use of hormonal contraceptives like the birth control pill simply for cycle regulation will eliminate potential side effects such as nausea, weight gain, spotting between periods, migraines, and moodiness. Avoiding the use of hormonal birth control can also lead to improved health in the longer term as the pill and other hormonal contraceptives have been associated with increased risks for heart disease and stroke [2], blood clots [3], bone density loss and osteoporosis [4, 5], breast cancer [6, 7, 8], and depression [9].

Emotionally Healthier Cycles

For some girls, not knowing when to expect their period can lead to anxiety. And cycles are typically most irregular during the teenage years. When teens are first getting used to dealing with their period, they may not feel comfortable sleeping over at a friend's house, going swimming, going camping, or wearing light-colored clothing. These perfectly normal feelings usually improve as girls gain confidence in knowing how to use and when to change their feminine hygiene products. However, girls with irregular cycles may have more difficultly planning events and gaining that confidence. With the knowledge gained from cycle awareness, even girls with extremely irregular cycles can have high confidence in predicting when their period will start. Being prepared for a period can improve self-confidence and self-esteem.

For most girls, whether we like to admit it or not, premenstrual symptoms (also known as PreMenstrual Syndrome, or PMS) can sometimes get the better of our emotions. Whether we become more sad and tearful or more jumpy and irritable, we often don't realize (or want to admit) that our emotional state is hormonally charged until after our period arrives and we look back in retrospect. Having an awareness of where you are in your cycle on any given day can help you better recognize when your emotions may be related to premenstrual hormones. And increased awareness can help you better handle what comes your way.

10

Brooke's story

When I was a teen, my cycles varied from about 32 days to about 60 days and anywhere in between. This meant there were several times when I spent an entire month thinking my period could literally start any minute. I wore a panty-liner every single day, never wore white pants, ran to the bathroom at the slightest sensation of moisture in my underwear, and often avoided swimming situations, even though I grew up in Florida. If I had known how to predict when my period would arrive or when the sensation of moisture in my underwear was most likely due to cervical mucus and not blood, my anxiety through my entire teenage years would have been greatly diminished.

Spiritually Healthier Cycles

Okay, so perhaps you're convinced, or at least curious to learn more about how understanding your natural cycles can help you lead a healthier life physically and emotionally, but spiritually? All I can say is, "Give it try". How God calls and connects with each girl, each person, is completely different but many women who have learned to chart their natural cycles say it has given them a greater appreciation for God's design of their body. By learning a small piece of the complex design of this world, we can glimpse the greatness of God's creation. Living life chastely and respecting God's natural design for your body can lead to awe and respect for God.

Each cycle, instead of dreading your period and wondering when it will come, you can know when it will start by interpreting the unique signs God gave you to understand your own body. When your period then arrives as your chart predicted, many girls experience a sense of amazement in knowing "My body is functioning as God intended." An appreciation for God's intricate design of our biology can remind us to observe and appreciate God's intricate designs in nature as we walk through the park on a fall day, in astronomy as we look up at the stars at night, in our relationships as we comfort a friend, and in many other aspects of our lives. You never know where you might encounter God.

Understanding and predicting your natural cycles may also help some girls in their goal to remain chaste. Although some girls begin taking birth control to regulate their cycles and not to prevent pregnancy, knowing the chances of pregnancy are low may increase the temptation to engage in sex before marriage. Remaining off birth control may reduce this temptation and act as a reminder to girls that sex is intimately connected with the possibility of conceiving new life. Girls who desire chastity before marriage but occasionally find themselves tempted to stray from this belief may find that understanding their natural cycles increases their spiritual resolve and connects them closer to God.

Healthier Future

Do you desire to get married one day? Some young girls dream of their wedding day and many teenage girls and young women hope to one day meet their soul mate. If or when you are called to marriage, you probably want to enter into that marriage with the expectation that it will be a healthy, happy, and permanent marriage.

Studies show that married couples using Natural Family Planning (NFP) have happier marriages and lower divorce rates [10]. Likewise, studies show that couples who wait until marriage to live together and have sex have a lower divorce rate [11].

Natural Family Planning is fertility awareness and involves charting and interpreting a woman's cycle signs to determine the fertile and infertile phases of her cycle. Knowing when the woman is potentially fertile, married couples using NFP can prayerfully decide to be sexually intimate during a woman's fertile phase to try to achieve a pregnancy or to abstain from sex during the fertile phase to postpone a pregnancy. NFP can be used to avoid pregnancy with an effectiveness of 99.6% [12], which is similar to that of hormonal birth control methods. But more importantly, using NFP to avoid or achieve pregnancy within marriage respects the bodies of the spouses, encourages tenderness between them, and fosters openness to life and love.

Since the primary purpose of NFP is to determine the fertile and infertile times, couples usually learn NFP when they are married or engaged to be married and will soon have a need to use NFP to either avoid or achieve a pregnancy. For an unmarried chaste teenage girl or young woman, learning specific rules to determine the fertile and infertile times in her cycle is unnecessary. But, as detailed in this chapter, learning to observe her body's cycle signs can lead to better health physically, emotionally, and spiritually. And young women shouldn't have to wait until marriage to understand what is going on in their bodies every day.

During this single phase of your womanhood, you can benefit from healthier cycles and grow in appreciation of God's natural design with the knowledge of cycle awareness. And quite possibly girls who learn to observe their cycles naturally before marriage will be more likely to desire to learn and use NFP in their marriage, which will not only help keep them healthier but will help keep their marriage healthier, too.

13

If you've heard NFP doesn't work, first know that modern methods of NFP are not the same as the "rhythm method" of the 1960s. Modern methods are based on each individual woman's cycle signs each day rather than on a "standard" cycle calendar. But you can also rest assured that learning your own body's natural signs does not commit you to use NFP in the future. In fact, by giving charting a try during your chaste unmarried years, you're not committed to anything (no side effects, no long term impacts, nothing irreversible). And perhaps by becoming familiar with your own body's natural signs, learning to interpret them to accurately predict your period, and gaining an awareness of all phases of your cycle, you may even begin to see how a natural method of planning and postponing pregnancies in the future may make sense after all.

Chapter 1 Summary

- Understanding your cycles through charting can help improve a girl's health physically, emotionally, and spiritually and help prepare for a healthy future.

- Cycle awareness can improve physical health by encouraging girls to:
  - Eat healthier
  - Develop better sleep habits
  - Exercise
  - Maintain a healthy body weight
  - Seek help for true medical issues
  - Try natural methods to manage symptoms
  - Avoid artificial hormones to regulate cycles

- Cycle awareness can improve emotional health by:
  - Reducing stress regarding when your period will start
  - Improving confidence in dealing with your cycles
  - Increasing self-esteem and body confidence
  - Raising awareness of cycle-related emotions

- Cycle awareness can improve spiritual health by:
  - Revealing God's amazing design of your own body
  - Increasing appreciation of God's design for your life
  - Helping solidify your resolve to live chastely

- Learning to chart your cycles as a teenager or young woman may encourage you to consider using Natural Family Planning during marriage which can lead to:
  - Happier marriages
  - Lower divorce rates
  - Avoiding or achieving pregnancy naturally

"So turn from youthful desires and pursue righteousness, faith, love, and peace, along with those who call on the Lord with purity of heart."
2 Timothy 2:22

Chapter 2:
Created Female

Why did God create women? In our modern society, we know women are capable of many noble feats including leading a country, helping alleviate world hunger, finding cures for diseases, teaching children, nurturing the sick, and caring for a family household. Perhaps you can discern your own personal life calling, or put it in perspective, by pondering God's design for woman and His instructions to all people. In this chapter, let's get ready to think about the mechanisms of the female reproductive system by contemplating God's creation of the very first woman and how God desires us to love ourselves and one another.

God's Design for Woman

To understand why God made women, we look back to the story of creation in the Bible. After forming man, God said "It is not good for the man to be alone." (Genesis 2:18) [13]. He desired man to have a helper, a supportive and nurturing companion. God made woman from the flesh of the man's flesh (Genesis 2:23). Man and woman were made for one another.

God created male and female both in His own image (Genesis 1:27). Man and woman are similar and with equal dignity. Though man and woman do have differences, their differences are complementary. Woman complements man and man complements woman physically, emotionally, and spiritually. We can see by the male and female anatomy that God designed man and woman complementary physically, to fit together in sexual union. In marriage, God unites man and woman to become "one body" (Genesis 2:24). God intends the companionship between man and woman in marriage to be helpful to one another, supportive and nurturing to each other, and loving and respectful of one another (Ephesians 5:33).

The sexual union between man and woman can bring about human life (Genesis 1:28). When a man and a woman have a child, the child is a genetic combination of the man and woman that reveals their living image and can help them realize their humanity as man and woman, father and mother [14]. God's instruction to "be fruitful and multiply" calls us not only to bring about new life but to do so in a manner consistent with God's love for us and His creation of mankind. To live, to love God, to love one another, and to bring about new life in Christ through this love helps us fulfill God's desires for humankind [15].

Does this mean that all women are called to marriage and motherhood? Each woman has her own unique gifts from God (1 Corinthians 7:7). And her gifts are suited to her vocation [14]. So while God designed woman with the capability to have children, some girls may become mothers and others may not. Each girl can prayerfully discern her own calling as a woman and live it to the fullest in Christ.

Whether or not each particular girl is called to become a mother, God's design for the female body is to have the capability of carrying a new life inside her womb. As one of the major differences between man and woman physically, we seek to understand and appreciate this distinction. God's design for a woman's body to aid in conceiving and nourishing a child during pregnancy reveals her femininity [14]. Beginning with puberty, a woman's body prepares for pregnancy and continues to prepare for pregnancy in cycles throughout the woman's fertile years. By God's own intricate design, the fertile time of a woman's cycle (the time in which she could become pregnant) is only a few days out of each cycle. In each cycle, God designed a phase of preparation for pregnancy, a phase of fertility, a phase for potentially fostering new life, and a phase for renewal for the next cycle. In His infinite wisdom and forethought, God gave woman physical signs that allow her to understand the phases of her cycles. By comprehending God's design for a woman's cycles, it offers us a glimpse of God's design for a woman's body and God's design for woman.

God's Design for Love

Man and woman were made for each other to be helpmates and companions, complementary to each other. In marriage, God unites man and woman in an intimate partnership. He not only calls husbands and wives to love one another but gives them an example of *how* to love one another.

In spreading the message of Jesus, Paul writes to the Ephesians regarding wives and husbands, "Be subordinate to one another out of reverence for Christ" (Ephesians 5:21). God, speaking through Paul, calls spouses to serve each other with mutual respect. He goes on to compare the relationship and love of husbands and wives to that of Christ and the church, His people (Ephesians 5:22-30). God desires husband and wife to love each other as He loves us.

During his time on earth, Jesus commanded us "love one another as I love you" (John 15:12). So *how* does Jesus love us? Jesus demonstrated His love for us by dying on the cross. The sacrifice of God's own Son is the perfect manifestation of God's love for His people. Pope John Paul II, a great theologian for all Christians, points out that Christ's love for us was given freely, totally, faithfully, and fruitfully [14]. In other words, Christ died on the cross for us by His own choosing and with full knowledge (John 10:11-18, John 13:3); He gave His body as a total gift, completely unselfishly, in service to His people (John 13:4-15); Christ's sacrifice of earthly life was faithful and everlasting and, through His resurrection and the gift of the Holy Spirit, His presence with us now is also everlasting (Matthew 28:20); and Christ's outpouring of love for us was fruitful in that it gave us abundant life (John 10:10, John 14:19-20) [16]. The love between husbands and wives in marriage should demonstrate these same attributes.

The mutual love between husband and wife should mirror the love of Christ to His people. "For this reason a man shall leave [his] father and [his] mother and be joined to his wife, and the two shall become one flesh. This is a great mystery, but I speak in reference to Christ and the church" (Ephesians 5:31-32). Here, God explains to us through Paul that not only should the emotional love of spouses demonstrate Christ's love for us but also that the "one flesh" physical joining of spouses should spiritually reflect the love between Christ and His church [14].

In marriage, the sexual intimacy of husband and wife is not only physical but also becomes a sign of their spiritual intimacy. In marriage, God desires that husband and wife are sexually intimate by their choice, that sex is unselfish and a total self-gift, that it signifies an everlasting and permanent union (Matthew 19:6), and that it is open to fruitful life. Sex in marriage is meant to express God's divine love for His people [14].

God's Desire for Chastity
Through Paul's first letter to the Corinthians, Christ instructs us to "Avoid immorality" and to "glorify God in your body" (1 Corinthians 6:18-20). With our understanding of God's design for marriage, we can see these instructions as more than strict rules to follow. Understanding how sex within marriage mirrors Christ's love for us, we can better see that sex outside of marriage cannot be love the way God intends. Sex outside of marriage brings only physical pleasure and

does not work toward spiritual communion with God. It is not an unselfish total gift, does not signify permanence, and is usually not intended to be life-giving. On the other hand, refraining from sex until marriage prepares men and women to be able to totally give themself to their spouse in marriage.

Chastity is a moral virtue, the act of living a sexually pure life. God desires all people in all states of life (not just the unmarried) to live chastely. Unmarried men and women are called to exhibit chastity by refraining from sex. Married men and women are called to exhibit chastity by saving all intimate thoughts only for each other (Matthew 5:27-28). Some religious people profess celibacy, allowing them to devote themselves solely to God alone. Living chastely, or sexually pure, means valuing God's design for our sexuality and giving it freely only in a manner that reflects Christ's love.

For some girls, abstaining from sex before marriage is truly a challenge and means giving up something they really want. Reasons some girls may refrain from sex are to avoid pregnancy, to avoid sexually transmitted disease, to follow the Bible or Church teachings, or because their parents taught them it was the right thing. While these are all great reasons to wait until marriage to have sex (either for the first time or again), simply saving sex for marriage for these reasons doesn't make your decision pleasing to God. Christ desires us to live a sexually pure life because we love Him so much that we want to reciprocate His love for us, not because we believe we have to or we should. To wait to have sex in marriage when you can give yourself completely to your spouse as an expression of God's love demonstrates your understanding of the great worth and significance of sex [15].

In our modern culture, is chastity realistic? There are influences against sexual integrity in television, movies, magazines, books, fashion, the internet, and social media. But living a sexually pure life is possible with commitment and prayer and by continually examining the amazing love of Christ demonstrated for His people – for *you*.

Recognize your dignity – you are worthy of honor and respect. Consider how avoiding situations of sexual temptation may prevent you from having to make tough decisions. In questions of sexual morality, ask yourself if this love you desire to give or receive images Christ's love. Is it free, total, faithful, and fruitful? In times when your physical or emotional desires try to convince you that the answers to these questions are "yes" when your spirit knows the truth, evaluate what your perspective will be on that particular act after the matter.

Will you have regret? Of teenagers in the United States who have had sex, 58% of them were unsure they really wanted it to occur [1]. How will you feel about that experience several years down the road when you are ready to truly and fully demonstrate Christ's love to your future spouse?

For additional inspiration in living out chastity, consider Mary. The young, virgin Mary's chaste and immaculate heart allowed her to whole-heartedly say "yes" to God when He called her (Luke 1:38). In the times we need encouragement to remain chaste, we can admire Mary and pray that our appreciation of God's love for us will change our hearts so that we desire to love as Christ loves.

God's Forgiveness
Perhaps you have been committed to saving sex for marriage since you first learned about puberty, perhaps you are still unsure of your decision to wait until marriage, or perhaps you have already had sex before marriage. Wherever you are at the moment, it is not too late to consider what God wants for your life going forward. You can commit or recommit yourself to chastity and loving as God loves you.

And God does love you unconditionally. God desires use to live morally. When we do not, are truly repentant, and desire to sin no more, He is ready to forgive us. God is love (1 John 4:8). God forgives our sins in baptism (Mark 16:16) and through repentance (Luke 24:47) and reconciliation with God (2 Corinthians 5:18). No sin is too great for God to forgive (Matthew 18:21-22). Anyone who is truly repentant and seeks God's forgiveness can be reconciled with God.

This book is intended for young women who are committed to abstaining from sex before marriage. Even if you have had sex in the past or have considered it a possibility if it felt "right" in the future, consider how God desires you to live your life going forward. If you can commit to waiting for sex only in marriage in order to love as God loves, then learning to chart your cycles with this book can reveal amazing things about the body God created just for you.

Chapter 2 Summary

- Understanding God's design for woman, God's design for love, and God's desire for chastity can help put in perspective why the female body functions as it does.

- God designed woman:
    - In His own image
    - As a companion for man
    - To complement man physically, emotionally, and spiritually
    - To conceive, carry, and nourish new life in the womb

- God's plan for marriage includes:
    - Husband and wife loving each other as Jesus loves us:
        - Freely
        - Totally
        - Faithfully
        - Fruitfully
    - A "one flesh" union that is both physically and spiritually intimate

- God's desire for chastity means God wants us to live a sexually pure life. Before marriage, chastity includes:
    - Sexual abstinence
    - Resisting situations of sexual temptation
    - Recognizing your dignity to be loved as God loves

- God forgives our sins in baptism and through repentance and reconciliation. You can commit or recommit yourself to saving sex for marriage to love as God loves.

- *Cycles & Spirituality* is intended for young women who are committed to abstaining from sex before marriage.

"You formed my inmost being; you knit me in my mother's womb. I praise you, so wonderfully you made me; wonderful are your works! My very self you knew; my bones were not hidden from you, When I was being made in secret, fashioned as in the depths of the earth. Your eyes foresaw my actions; in your book all are written down; my days were shaped before one came to be. How precious to me are your designs, O God; how vast the sum of them! Were I to count, they would outnumber the sands; to finish, I would need eternity."
Psalm 139:13-18

Chapter 3:
How My Body Creates My Cycle Signs

In Part II, you'll learn how measuring your temperature and observing your cervical mucus can reveal where you are in your cycle on any given day. Charting these signs will help you notice how they change from day to day – how your own temperature rises and how your own mucus changes. But first, in Chapter 3, let's learn what causes these physical changes by examining God's intricate design for the female reproductive organs and how hormones trigger the observable signs that allow us insight into our bodies.

Sarah's story
When I first learned about the female anatomy, I was about 10 and had not started my period. I found the whole discussion awkward and uncomfortable. Now that I am older and dealing with my period is not so foreign, I appreciate learning about my anatomy again. I can comprehend God's design in a whole new light instead of only worrying about what bleeding will be like.

My Anatomy and My Cycles

If you could look inside your body, here are the main organs you would find as part of your reproductive system. The ovaries produce eggs and typically release one egg each cycle. Most girls have two ovaries, one on the left and one on the right side of the body. The Fallopian tubes transport the eggs to your uterus. There are two Fallopian tubes, one on the left and one on the right side of your body. In the uterus, also known as your womb, a fertilized egg can implant to allow a baby to grow. The lining of the uterus is the endometrium. The cervix is an internal organ near the opening of the vagina that helps protect a growing baby. The vagina is the canal that extends from the cervix to the vaginal opening. The external female organs at the vaginal opening include the labia (folds of skin surrounding the vaginal opening) and the clitoris (the sensitive external erectile organ) and are collectively called the vulva.

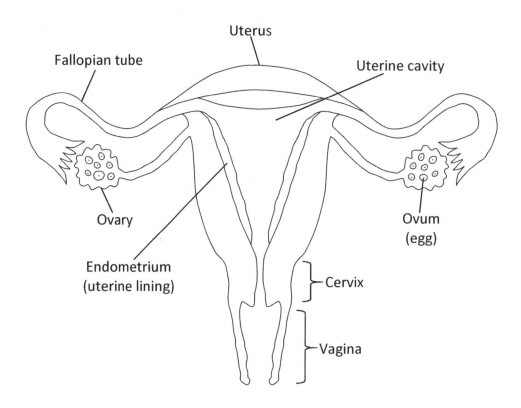

Internal Female Anatomy

In the first part of a menstrual cycle, the endometrium (lining of the uterus) is shed during days of bleeding. This shedding and bleeding is called menstruation. A typical menstruation lasts 3-7 days [17] and includes days of heavy or normal bleeding and days of lighter bleeding. After menstruation, the lining of the uterus begins to build back up in order to be ready for the implantation of a new life if an egg is fertilized. This replenishment of the endometrium typically occurs over 1-2 weeks but can vary from girl to girl and even from cycle to cycle. This phase of the menstrual cycle is called the follicular phase.

Around mid-cycle, one of the ovaries matures an egg and releases it. This is called ovulation.

The egg then travels through the Fallopian tube to the uterus over a timeframe of around 7-10 days. If the egg has been fertilized by sperm from a male, it can then implant in the lining of the uterus to continue to grow new life. If the egg has not been fertilized, it will be shed along with the endometrium during the next menstruation. The time between ovulation and the next menstruation is called the luteal phase.

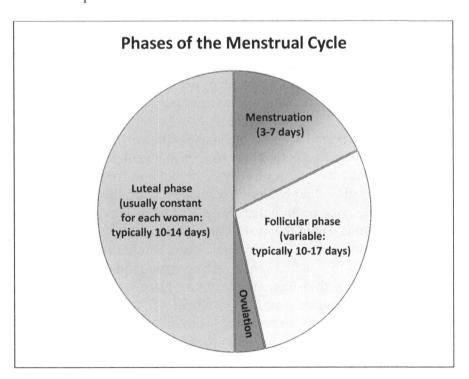

The first day of menstrual bleeding is considered the first day of a new cycle. To determine the total length of your cycle, count the number of days from the first day of menstrual bleeding to the day before your next period starts. The length of a menstrual cycle varies from girl to girl and often from cycle to cycle. The average length of an adult menstrual cycle is 21-35 days, however longer or shorter cycles may not be abnormal. Younger women and girls may have even more variability with a typical menstrual cycle length of 21-45 days [18]. Our modern society has designated 28 days as the "standard" length of a menstrual cycle with ovulation occurring on day 14 of the cycle. It turns out, however, that only 14% of women have a "standard" cycle [19]! For teenage girls and younger women, the percentage is even lower. So the vast majority of young women have a "non-standard" cycle length.

Variability in the length of the follicular phase accounts for most variations in total cycle length [20]. This means that if the length of your cycle varies from cycle to cycle, it is mostly likely because your body is taking a different amount of its own sweet time to prepare for ovulation and build up the lining of the uterus. The length of the luteal phase is typically stable for each girl. This means that if you can identify when ovulation has occurred each cycle, the length of time from ovulation until your period is usually the same from cycle to cycle for each girl. A typical luteal phase length is around 10-14 days for most women but only varies by a day or two for each individual woman. As you learn to observe your own body's signs, the stable length of the luteal phase is the important feature that allows you to predict when your period will occur.

A girl's very first menstrual period is called menarche. The typical age of menarche is 11-14 [17] but your first period may happen at a younger or older age. After menarche, a girl's next several cycles may be irregular in length with some very long cycles or some rather short cycles. Irregular cycle lengths following menarche are most likely caused by anovulatory cycles. In an anovulatory cycle, the lining of the uterus builds up but the ovaries do not release an egg. Eventually, the endometrium is shed and bleeding occurs before the endometrium is excessively thickened, even though ovulation did not take place. Bleeding that occurs even though ovulation did not take place is called breakthrough bleeding. The average time between a girl's first period and when she begins having ovulatory cycles that are more "regular" in length is approximately 14-24 months but varies based on the length of time since menarche and the age at menarche. Some girls may experience ovulatory cycles during the first year following menarche or even the first cycle and some girls may still experience anovulatory cycles three to twelve years following menarche [17, 19].

As girls transition from anovulatory to ovulatory cycles, ovulation may occur a few days later in the cycle for teen girls and young women, compared to the typical ovulatory cycles of older women, resulting in overall longer cycles [17]. Cycle lengths usually become shorter and more regular for women ages 25-35.

My Hormones and How They Create Observable Signs

A girl's menstrual cycle is a result of hormones. Although it has become cliché to say girls can be "hormonal", it is truly quite literal! Hormones are like chemical messengers that give signals to parts of your body. Four hormones play a major role in your menstrual cycle. Follicle Stimulating Hormone (FSH) and Luteinizing Hormone (LH) are produced in the brain. Estrogen and progesterone are produced in the female reproductive organs. These four hormones signal the female reproductive organs to produce the observable signs you will learn to chart to understand your cycles.

In the beginning of each new cycle, the brain releases FSH. This hormone signals the ovaries to prepare and mature an egg. Around the same time, the reproductive organs increase production of estrogen. Estrogen signals the glands in the cervix to produce mucus, promotes mucus flow to the vulva, softens and slightly opens the cervix, and builds up the lining of the uterus [16, 21]. All of these physical changes occur in preparation for the possibility of an egg to be fertilized by sperm to produce new life. But they also produce observable signs of approaching ovulation. Wow at God's foresight!

The phase of the cycle during which FSH causes the ovaries to mature an egg and estrogen prepares the uterus, cervix, and cervical mucus to act as a friendly habitat for sperm is the follicular phase. The follicular phase can last from several days to a few weeks and may vary from cycle to cycle in each girl.

Near the end of the follicular phase, the brain increases production of LH. This hormone travels to the ovary and signals the ovary to release the mature egg. The release of the mature egg, or ovum, is called ovulation.

After ovulation, the reproductive organs then increase production of the fourth important hormone, progesterone. This hormone signals the glands in the cervix to thicken, dry up, or stop producing cervical mucus; signals the cervix to close and harden; continues to enrich the endometrium; and causes the resting body temperature to rise [16, 21]. All of these physical changes occur to help protect any new life that may have been conceived and prevent any further ovulations during that cycle. Many of these physical changes also produce observable signs that help us know ovulation has passed and when to anticipate the start of a period if pregnancy did not occur.

After ovulation, levels of FSH and LH decrease dramatically, levels of estrogen decrease slightly, but levels of progesterone remain elevated for the remainder of the cycle. The time around ovulation is certainly a time of hormone fluctuation! And as we know from societal clichés, a "hormonal" girl can experience a wide variety of emotions. Understanding when ovulation is approaching and has passed can better help you understand the impacts on your own well-being.

If pregnancy did not occur, progesterone levels drop at the beginning of the next cycle when the brain sends a signal to shed the lining of the uterus and begin to prepare again for the possibility of new life.

The next two graphs visually show approximate relative levels of estrogen, progesterone, FSH, and LH at various times during a menstrual cycle [21]. These graphs use a 28-day cycle for convenience but cycle lengths can vary from girl to girl and even from cycle to cycle. In cycles that are shorter or longer than 28 days, the length of time for estrogen, FSH, and LH to reach their highest levels (the follicular phase) will vary but the length of time from ovulation to the start of the next period (the luteal phase) will remain approximately the same for each girl.

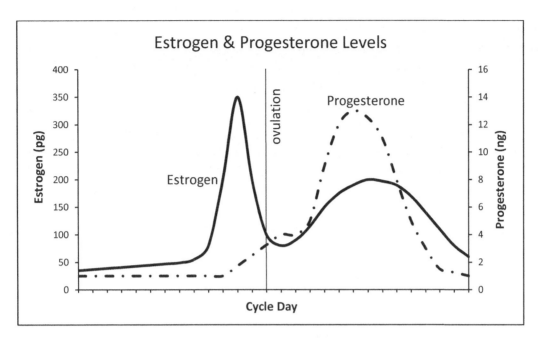

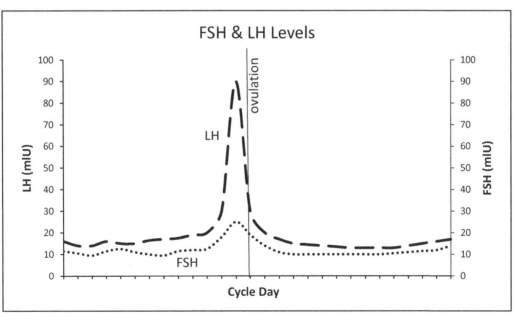

Understanding this simplistic overview of the four key female reproductive hormones highlights a few important points:

1) A girl's hormones are constantly fluctuating! Take a look at a combined graph showing the relative levels of the four primary hormones all together. Notice that there are no two days in the entire cycle where a girl's hormones are *exactly* the same! This emphasizes how complex and intricate God's design is. But understanding how these fluctuating hormones impact *you*, personally, can better help each girl learn to have healthier cycles physically, emotionally, and even spiritually.

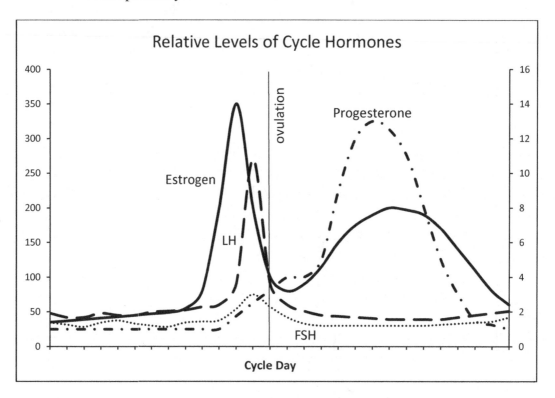

2) Each hormone in a girl's body plays a critical role in the changes that occur in her body during her cycle, and many of these changes create physical and observable signs that most girls can detect. Though God's design is complex and intricate, in His infinite wisdom, He gave us these signs to assist us on our journey through life. Learning to recognize your own body's signs can help each girl know when ovulation is approaching and know when to expect her period to start.

Chapter 3 Summary

- The female reproductive hormones create observable signs to help you understand your cycle.

- A menstrual cycle starts on the first day of your period.

- The phases of the menstrual cycle are:
    o Menstruation
    o Follicular Phase
    o Ovulation
    o Luteal Phase

- Cycle lengths can vary and are not 28 days in all girls.
    o Variability in cycle lengths is primarily due to variability in the length of the follicular phase.
    o Each girl typically has the same luteal phase length each cycle.
        ▪ A consistent luteal phase length helps predict when your period will start.

- A girl's first several cycles may be non-ovulatory.
    o Bleeding may be "breakthrough bleeding" instead of menstruation.

- The four hormones that affect the female reproductive system are:
    o FSH
    o Estrogen
    o LH
    o Progesterone

- Hormone levels change throughout the entire cycle.
    o Changing hormones help create observable signs (including cervical mucus and waking body temperature) to help understand when ovulation is approaching and when to predict your period.

Part II:
Understanding God's Design of My Body

Perhaps with the previous overview of the female body you can begin to appreciate that God's design for women is intricate and sophisticated. Each cycle, various hormones surge and decline to prepare the womb, release an egg, anticipate fertilization, and either help sustain a new human being or prepare again for the next cycle. All of this happens inside your body regardless of if you are cognizant of it or not. Now let's discuss how these happenings inside your body affect physical and visible signs you can observe. Your hormones create mucus at the opening of your cervix that changes in composition, appearance, and feel throughout your cycle. And your hormones affect your resting body temperature in a measureable way. If that sounds bizarre or complicated, don't worry. Part II will specifically describe the signs (Chapter 4), how to begin noticing them (Chapter 5), and what they tell you about the various phases of your cycle, including how to predict when your period will arrive (Chapter 6). And after only one full cycle, you may already begin to feel more comfortable with your own body's hints and start to see interesting patterns.

"Beloved, I hope you are prospering in every respect and are in good health, just as your soul is prospering."
3 John 1:2

Chapter 4:
The Signs God Gave Me

In *Cycles & Spirituality*, the primary signs you will learn to observe are your cervical mucus and your waking basal body temperature. As you make daily observations of these signs on your own personal chart, they will begin to reveal a pattern.

Cervical Mucus

Each cycle, as your body prepares to release an egg and estrogen levels rise, your cervix produces mucus. You may have noticed this mucus as a white, yellow, or clear fluid in your underwear. Or perhaps you have noticed a slippery feeling when you wipe after going to the bathroom. Society has accepted the term "discharge" which gives the unfortunate connotation of an unwanted secretion. But, in fact, cervical mucus is a clean and healthy fluid your body naturally produces in response to hormones. Instead of being embarrassed by "discharge", take a second to look closer and you'll discover that the changes in your cervical mucus are God's creative clue to you about what is happening in your cycle.

Near the beginning of each cycle, the cervix typically does not produce mucus. As estrogen levels rise, your cervix begins to make mucus that is thick, creamy, pasty, opaque, crumbly, sticky, tacky, or gooey. Over a few days, as ovulation approaches, it changes to become thin, clear, watery, stretchy, or like raw egg whites. After ovulation, cervical mucus begins to dry up or return to the gooey state.

The changes to cervical mucus help denote the phases of your cycle. With practice, you will be able to observe your cervical mucus during your regular visits to the restroom. As you keep track of them on your chart, you will notice a pattern. This pattern is unique to you and your own body and it is unique to each of your own cycles. The cervical mucus pattern will be your clue of approaching ovulation. And recognizing signs of ovulation will help you understand how hormones may be impacting you and help you predict your period.

Basal Body Temperature

Your basal body temperature is the lowest temperature your body reaches during rest. After ovulation, your body begins to release progesterone, which causes your basal body temperature to rise by about four tenths of a degree Fahrenheit (0.4°F) and remain elevated until the start of your next period. A good time to measure your basal body temperature is at the same time each day immediately after awakening from sleep in the morning before any physical activity.

Before you panic, a basal body temperature can easily be measured orally under your tongue with a digital thermometer! It may also be measured vaginally but this is not necessary. An oral temperature measurement provides enough accuracy to observe the temperature rise.

You may be surprised to learn that a normal basal body temperature is typically well below the average active human body temperature of 98.6°F. In the first half of your cycle, typical basal body temperatures range from about 97.2 to 97.6°F and in the second half of your cycle, typical basal body temperatures range from about 97.9 to 98.4°F.

The Pattern

Observing only your cervical mucus and your basal body temperature together will give you enough information to determine the phases of your cycle. You will be able to determine when ovulation has occurred and then predict when to expect your period. As you gain experience charting your cycle signs, you may also notice other hints or clues your own unique body gives you around the time of ovulation. With each new cycle, you will be able to observe the signs God gave you and how they create a pattern to reveal what is going on in your own individual body. Since each cycle you chart is based on the signs you observe that cycle, you will have real-time insight into your body for that moment in time, not an approximation based on your past history or on the idea of an average "standard" cycle.

When to Get Started

The best time to get started charting with *Cycles & Spirituality* is about 1 to 2 years or more after you first start your periods. This will give you some time to get comfortable with the basics of caring for your body during your period and using feminine hygiene products before taking on the additional task of charting. It will also allow your body time for cycles to become ovulatory. For girls who reached menarche before age 12, cycles are sometimes ovulatory within the first year. For girls who reached menarche after age 12, it may take two or more years for cycles to become regularly ovulatory [17, 19].

However, if you're excited to start charting earlier, give it a try! Just be prepared that your mucus and temperature signs may not show a typical pattern if you are not yet ovulating every cycle and you may have some cycles with a "period" (actually breakthrough bleeding) not predicted by your chart.

Whenever you decide to start charting, it is not necessary to wait for the beginning of a new cycle to begin making observations of your body's natural signs.

Getting Started
To get started, you need:
- o   A basal body thermometer
- o   A *Cycles & Spirituality* chart

Modern basal body thermometers are digital and can be purchased at drugstores or superstores. Just be certain it says "basal" as basal thermometers are more accurate in the temperature range of interest.

In order to visually see the patterns in your cervical mucus and temperature each cycle, you'll have to write it down. Perhaps keeping a daily log sounds like a chore but if you give it a try, you'll probably find that it takes less than a minute a day and will reveal fascinating happenings in your own body.

Many apps and online charting software exist to try to help you analyze your cycles. But most of them are focused on fertility and analyzing your signs to determine your fertile and infertile phases for either postponing or achieving pregnancy. You may find this added information confusing and unnecessary if your intent is simply to gain awareness of your body's signs and how they may relate to your symptoms. Some apps and online charting programs try to predict your period but only gather information about your previous cycle history and cycle lengths, not about the current daily symptoms your own body reveals. If you decide to use existing apps, try to understand their main purpose and what data they use to interpret your cycles.

The *Cycles & Spirituality* chart designed specifically for this book focuses on the information relevant to teen girls and young women who are not sexually active and who simply want to understand their own cycles. Taking a look at the big picture of your own chart each cycle and interpreting it yourself will give you the most insight about your body and allow you to predict more accurately when your period will arrive. It will also help you observe trends in your own cycles and notice recurring symptoms that may be unique to you.

Let's look at the *Cycles & Spirituality* blank chart. You can also find the blank chart in Appendix C and at www.cyclesandspirituality.com.

CYCLES & Spirituality

Name _____ Age _____ Year _____ Chart # _____

My Typical Luteal Phase Length _____

Day of month

Month

Day of week

Date

Temperature (°F)

Normal Time I Measure Temperature: _____

Cycle Day: 1 2 3 4 5 6 7 8 9 10 11 12 13 14 15 16 17 18 19 20 21 22 23 24 25 26 27 28 29 30 31 32 33 34 35 36 37 38 39 40

Bleeding ● ◐ ○

Mucus
- wet / stretchy
- damp / gooey
- dry / none

Symptoms
- physical symptoms,
- moods,
- impacts

Care
- exercises,
- foods,
- vitamins,
- prayers

Cycles & Spirituality Blank Chart

To get started, fill out the top line of your chart with your name, your age, the date, and your chart number.

Name: Putting your name on your chart is optional but may help if you ever want to ask for advice on your chart, show your chart to your doctor, or have sisters who use the same chart and want to keep them separate.

My Typical Luteal Phase Length: We will discuss this section in detail later. Leave it blank until you have charted for at least 1 cycle.

Age: Writing your age on your chart will also help if you share your chart with someone for advice or if you want to look back on your charts historically and see how your cycles were different at various ages.

Year: Fill in with the current calendar year.

Chart #: If this is your first cycle charting your signs, start with chart #1. Advance the number for each subsequent cycle. Start a new chart on the first day of each menstrual period. (If you ever have a cycle that lasts longer than 40 days, begin a new chart and keep the same chart number but denote it with a letter. For example, if cycle #3 is 45 days long, start a new page for days 41-45. Label the first page Chart #3a and the second page Chart #3b.)

Day of Month: If the first day of your period falls on May 18th, then the corresponding day of the month is 18. Fill in the rest of the line with sequential numbers for the calendar days.

Month: Fill in the month in which your cycle begins. If the month changes mid-cycle, write in a new month name on the appropriate day.

Day of Week: If the first day of your period is Monday, then the corresponding day of the week on cycle day 1 is Monday. Fill in the rest of the line with abbreviations for the days of the week (S M T W R F S).

Below is an example of how to fill out the top few lines of your chart each cycle.

❦

Example # 1: Setting up a new chart

Abigail decides to begin her first chart on the first day of her next period, which begins on Monday, May 18, 2015. Here is how she should fill out her chart:

CYCLES & *Spirituality*																																							
Name _Abigail_ My Typical Luteal Phase Length _____ Age _16_ Year _20XX_ Chart # _1_																																							
Day of month	18	19	20	21	22	23	24	25	26	27	28	29	30	31	1	2	3	4	5	6	7	8	9	10	11	12	13	14	15	16	17	18	19	20	21	22	23	24	25	26
Month	May													June																										
Day of week	M	T	W	R	F	S	S	M	T	W	R	F	S	S	M	T	W	R	F	S	S	M	T	W	R	F	S	S	M	T	W	R	F	S	S	M	T	W	R	F

❦

42

When charting your cycles, cycle day 1 of each cycle is the first day of menstrual bleeding. Always start a new chart page on the first day of your period.

For your very first cycle charting, it is not necessary to wait for the first day of your period to begin observing your symptoms. If you happen know what day of your current cycle you are on, then start writing down your symptoms for that day. For example, if it has been 20 days since the first day of your last period, you are on cycle day 20 and can start writing down your signs on day 20 of chart #1. If you do not know exactly what day of your cycle you are on, just guess and start making observations. Though you may not be able to accurately interpret your signs for chart #1 if you begin charting mid-cycle, you can at least become familiar with observing the signs and writing them down. If you find this too confusing, wait for your next period and begin your first chart that day.

Chapter 4 Summary

- Observing your cervical mucus and basal body temperature can reveal a pattern that helps you determine the phases of your cycle.

- Cervical mucus is a healthy fluid your body naturally produces in response to hormones.
  - A typical cervical mucus pattern is:
    - No mucus for a few days following menstruation
    - Thick, creamy, pasty, opaque, sticky, tacky, or gooey mucus as estrogen rises
    - Thin, clear, watery, stretchy, or egg white mucus as ovulation approaches
    - No mucus or thick, creamy, pasty, opaque, sticky, tacky, or gooey mucus until the next menstruation

- Basal body temperature is the lowest temperature your body reaches during rest.
  - It is measured with a basal body thermometer under your tongue immediately after waking.
  - Basal body temperature rises around the time of ovulation and remains elevated during the luteal phase.

- You can start charting with *Cycles & Spirituality* after you have been getting your period for a year or two.
  - Use the chart in Appendix C.
  - Start a new chart on the first day of each period.

"I urge you therefore, brothers, by the mercies of God, to offer your bodies as a living sacrifice, holy and pleasing to God, your spiritual worship. Do not conform yourselves to this age but be transformed by the renewal of your mind, that you may discern what is the will of God, what is good and pleasing and perfect."
Romans 12:1-2

Chapter 5:
Observing My Own Signs

Are you finally ready to start observing your own body's signs? Here's what to look for when observing your bleeding, mucus, waking temperature, and other signs unique to you!

Observing My Bleeding

Begin a new chart on the first day of your period. Note your days of menstrual bleeding on the *Cycles & Spirituality* chart in the line labeled "Bleeding". Use the following symbols to note different days of bleeding:

    ● for days of normal or heavy bleeding
    ⊖ for days of light bleeding
    ○ for days of spotting

The next example shows how and where to record days of bleeding on your chart.

———————————————————— ✂ ————————————————————

Example # 2: Recording Bleeding

During her period, Abigail has heavy or normal blood flow on May 18 & 19 (cycle days 1-2), light blood flow on May 20 & 21 (cycle days 3-4), and spotting on May 22 (cycle day 5). On June 14 (cycle day 28), Abigail starts her next period and has normal blood flow. Here is how she should fill out the line for "Bleeding" on her chart:

CYCLES & *Spirituality*

Name ___Abigail___ My Typical Luteal Phase Length _____ Age _16_ Year _20XX_ Chart # _1_

Date	Day of month	18	19	20	21	22	23	24	25	26	27	28	29	30	31	1	2	3	4	5	6	7	8	9	10	11	12	13	14	15	16	17	18	19	20	21	22	23	24	25	26
	Month					May																			June																
	Day of week	M	T	W	R	F	S	S	M	T	W	R	F	S	S	M	T	W	R	F	S	S	M	T	W	R	F	S	S	M	T	W	R	F	S	S	M	T	W	R	F

Cycle Day	1	2	3	4	5	6	7	8	9	10	11	12	13	14	15	16	17	18	19	20	21	22	23	24	25	26	27	28	29	30	31	32	33	34	35	36	37	38	39	40
Bleeding ●⊖○	●	●	⊖	⊖	○																							●												

———————————————————— ✂ ————————————————————

Observing My Mucus
When menstrual flow begins to lessen each cycle (so, starting on days of light bleeding or spotting), become aware of any observations of cervical mucus.

Observe your cervical mucus by noticing how the mucus feels during the day, what the mucus looks like, and its characteristics when you touch it between your fingers (remember, cervical mucus is a clean and healthy fluid).

Sense & Feel
Start to become aware of how your cervical mucus feels as you go about your day. Notice the different sensations created by cervical mucus. Can you feel or sense it between your labia (without even looking) while you have underwear and clothes on during the day? When you go to the bathroom, can you feel or sense it at the opening of the vagina as you wipe with toilet paper? You may notice it when you wipe after urinating or when you wipe after a bowel movement.

As you become aware of the sense and feel of your cervical mucus, try to categorize it in one of the following descriptions:

> Dry
> Damp
> Wet

Dry means observing no other feelings or sensations of cervical mucus as you go about your day or as you wipe during bathroom visits. Other descriptions of feeling "dry" may include:
- Feeling rough or scratchy when wiping
- Feeling like the toilet paper meets with friction when wiping

Damp means observing feelings or sensations of dampness at the opening of your vagina as you go about your day or as you wipe during bathroom visits. Other descriptions of feeling "damp" may include:
- Feeling moist or humid
- Feeling sticky or like the labia stick together

Wet means observing feelings or sensations of wetness or of slipperiness at the opening of your vagina as you go about your day or as you wipe during bathroom visits. Other descriptions of feeling "wet" may include:

- Feeling watery, liquidy, or runny during the day
- Feeling like the toilet paper is slippery or glides across the opening of the vagina when wiping
- Feeling like you need to wipe more than once

If you sense and feel various kinds of mucus at different times during the same day, summarize the day with a description of the highest level of mucus. For example, if you feel dry most of the day but feel and sense dampness at one point or during one bathroom visit, consider it a "damp" day. If you feel sticky most of the day but have a sensation of wateriness for a short time, consider it a "wet" day.

The next example shows sample descriptions of cervical mucus sense and feel day-by-day during a cycle and shows how each description can be summarized as either dry, damp, or wet.

⚜

Example # 3: Describing Mucus Sense & Feel

Abigail observes the following ways her cervical mucus senses and feels as she goes about her day and when she wipes during bathroom visits. Each description of her mucus sense and feel is summarized on the right. On cycle days 1-2 she did not note mucus because her bleeding was heavy or normal flow.

Day	Description of Sense & Feel of Mucus	Summary
3	Blood flow was lighter than previous two days; did not observe any mucus	dry
4	Same as Day 3	dry
5	Some spotty blood, no mucus, felt dry throughout the day	dry
6	Felt dry most of the day but sensed dampness when wiping during one bathroom visit	damp
7	Felt dry all day and very dry when wiping at every bathroom visit	dry
8	Seemed humid during the day but still dry when wiping	damp
9	Felt damp off-and-on throughout the day and damp when wiping a few times	damp
10	Felt damp as walked around and moist when wiping, definitely not dry	damp
11	Seemed constantly sticky all day and moist when wiping at every bathroom visit	damp
12	Felt wet during the day and somewhat wet when wiping	wet
13	Wet during the day and wet a few times when wiping	wet
14	More wet throughout the day, toilet paper seemed to glide easily	wet
15	Wet all day and very wet when wiping	wet
16	Seemed very wet and felt slippery when wiping once	wet
17	Wet and very slippery when wiping	wet
18	Very wet and very slippery; felt the need to wipe more than once due to wetness	wet
19	Not wet anymore, just dampness throughout day; felt damp when wiping but definitely not slippery or wet like yesterday	damp
20	Felt dry during the day and dry when wiping	dry
21	Dry	dry
22	Felt dry all day and toilet paper met with friction when wiping	dry
23	Seemed damp at times during the day and toilet paper felt moist during one bathroom visit	damp
24	Dry all day; no dampness	dry
25	Dry	dry
26	Dry	dry
27	Dry	dry
28	Period started, normal amount of blood flow	

⚜

Writing down these detailed descriptions of your mucus each day is not necessary. This example is simply to demonstrate how your own descriptions would translate into a summary word for quick notation on your chart at the end of each day.

Although this observation of the sense & feel of your cervical mucus may seem elusive at first, you will likely become more aware of it as you continue to practice and gain familiarity with your body and mucus. It may encourage you to know that even blind women can become aware of the sense and feel of their mucus [22]!

See & Touch
Using your senses of sight and touch, notice what your cervical mucus looks like and how it responds when you touch it.

Ways to see your cervical mucus include gathering it up on your fingers from the opening of your vagina and looking at it on the toilet paper after you wipe. To gather up your cervical mucus, use clean fingers and gently swipe across the opening of the vagina and try to grasp some of your cervical mucus between your fingers. Use whatever technique works best for you – one finger, two fingers, or the thumb and one finger together – to draw the cervical mucus out of the vagina. Occasionally you may notice a stream of cervical mucus as it slips out of the vagina (often immediately after a bowel movement). Try to gather it up between your fingers for a closer look. You may also notice cervical mucus resting on the toilet paper after you wipe. In order to better observe and see mucus, some girls find it helpful to wipe with toilet paper folded flat or to wipe prior to urinating to avoid confusion between wetness on the toilet paper from urine versus from cervical mucus. Mucus typically "sits" on the surface of the toilet paper whereas urine soaks into the toilet paper. With your mucus either gathered between your fingers or resting on the toilet paper, notice how it looks. Notice the color, how opaque or clear it is, how thin or thick it looks, and any other way that makes sense to you to describe the visible appearance of the mucus.

While you have your cervical mucus gathered up between your fingers, use your sense of touch to observe its characteristics. If you used the toilet paper method as a way to visibly see your cervical mucus, now use your fingers to touch it and gather it up from the toilet paper. Rub the mucus between your thumb and middle finger and notice the texture. Then separate your thumb and middle finger slowly to try to pull apart and stretch the mucus. Observe whether or not it stretches and how easily it breaks. Attempt to stretch it a few times and observe if it stretches repeatedly or breaks.

Try to categorize the sight and texture of your cervical mucus in one of the following descriptions:

> None
> Gooey
> Stretchy

> **None** means you cannot see or touch any cervical mucus at all. It cannot be gathered up in your fingers by swiping across the vaginal opening or gathered up from the toilet paper after wiping.

> **Gooey** means the mucus may have a texture that is sticky, pasty, crumbly, tacky, gooey, or like rubber cement. The mucus may appear white, yellow, cloudy, chalky, milky, opaque, dense, or thick. If you try to stretch it, the mucus either breaks or cannot be stretched repeatedly without breaking.

> **Stretchy** means the mucus stretches when you pull it apart. It may only stretch an inch or may stretch several inches without breaking but is usually elastic and can be stretched repeatedly. The mucus may appear clear, translucent, thin, watery, runny, or like raw eggwhites.

If you see and touch various kinds of mucus during one day, summarize the day with a description of the highest level of mucus. For example, if you do not see and cannot gather up any mucus during most bathroom visits but then see a little bit of milky, thick mucus during one bathroom visit that day, consider it a "gooey" day. If you see and touch gooey mucus during most visits to the bathroom in one day and see and touch stretchy mucus during only one bathroom visit, consider it a "stretchy" day.

The next example shows sample descriptions of cervical mucus sight and texture day-by-day during a cycle and shows how each description can be summarized as either none, gooey, or stretchy.

Example # 4: Describing Mucus See & Touch

Abigail observes the following about her cervical mucus when she sees and touches it during bathroom visits. Each description of her mucus sight and texture is summarized on the right.

Day	Description of See & Touch of Mucus	Summary
3	Light blood flow but did not see any mucus	none
4	Lighter blood flow; still did not see any mucus	none
5	Some spotty blood; did not see any mucus on the toilet paper	none
6	No mucus; could not gather any up with fingertips at the vagina opening	none
7	No mucus present to see or touch	none
8	Did not see any mucus; no mucus on toilet paper	none
9	Saw mucus sitting on toilet paper; appeared milky; tried to pick up off toilet paper but too sticky and not enough to gather between fingers	gooey
10	Saw whitish-yellow mucus on toilet paper; looked sticky; picked it up off toilet paper and it was like rubber cement between fingers when pulled them apart – lots of strands that broke	gooey
11	Slightly more mucus on toilet paper; looked thick and opaque with some clear streaks; felt creamy when gathered it up between fingers	gooey
12	Mucus looked cloudy; did not stretch – too dense	gooey
13	During most bathroom visits, mucus appeared thick. But two times it was slightly thinner and more clear and could stretch it about ½"	stretchy
14	Mucus on toilet paper looked translucent; stretched ~1" between fingers	stretchy
15	Saw mucus on toilet paper – looked like raw eggwhites; stretched about 1"	stretchy
16	Noticed a string of mucus fall into toilet after a bowel movement before had the chance to gather it up; at other bathroom visits, saw thin and clear mucus on toilet paper, stretched a few inches	stretchy
17	Mucus was very thin and stringy, almost watery; stretched several inches	stretchy
18	Lots of clear and stretchy mucus	stretchy
19	Thicker mucus; clung to toilet paper every time tried to gather it up	gooey
20	Did not see any mucus; could not gather any mucus at vaginal opening	none
21	No mucus to see or touch	none
22	None	none
23	Tiny bit of gooey mucus on toilet paper once	gooey
24	No mucus	none
25	No mucus	none
26	Nothing	none
27	None	none
28	Period started	

Again, writing down these detailed descriptions of the cervical mucus you can see and touch is not necessary. This example is simply to demonstrate how your own descriptions would translate into a summary word for quick notation on your chart at the end of each day.

Recording Mucus

The cervix produces many different kinds of mucus [23]. For *Cycles & Spirituality*, you can summarize mucus into three main types: dry/none, damp/gooey, and wet/stretchy. At the end of each day, think about your mucus observations (both what you could sense & feel and what you could see & touch) throughout the entire day. Fill in the corresponding box in the "Mucus" section of your chart to summarize your descriptions.

If you sensed and felt dry and you saw and touched nothing, color in the box labeled "dry/none". Likewise, if you sensed and felt damp and saw and touched gooey mucus, color in the box labeled "damp/gooey". If you sensed and felt wet and saw and touched stretchy mucus, color in the box labeled "wet/stretchy".

Your description of sense & feel and see & touch may not always match up perfectly. With practice, you may be able to sense and feel mucus before you can actually see and touch it. In cases where your descriptions do not match, fill in the highest box on the chart that matches one of your descriptions. For example, if you sensed and felt damp but could not see or touch anything, color in the box for "damp/gooey" since it is higher on the chart than the box for "dry/none". If you sensed and felt wet but when you gathered up the mucus and tried to stretch it, it broke easily and seemed gooey, color in the higher box for "wet/stretchy". By recording the highest level of mucus you observe, you will become more in tune with the various changes and phases of your cycle.

For extra practice, use a blank *Cycles & Spirituality* chart to record the overall mucus observations for Abigail from her descriptions of mucus sense & feel in Example # 3 and her descriptions of mucus see & touch in Example # 4. The answer follows in Example # 5.

54

Example # 5: Recording Mucus

Abigail records her mucus observations on her chart at the end of each day.

CYCLES & *Spirituality*

Name __Abigail__   My Typical Luteal Phase Length _____   Age __16__   Year __20XX__   Chart # __1__

Date		18	19	20	21	22	23	24	25	26	27	28	29	30	31	1	2	3	4	5	6	7	8	9	10	11	12	13	14	15	16	17	18	19	20	21	22	23	24	25	26
	Day of month	18	19	20	21	22	23	24	25	26	27	28	29	30	31	1	2	3	4	5	6	7	8	9	10	11	12	13	14	15	16	17	18	19	20	21	22	23	24	25	26
	Month					May																	June																		
	Day of week	M	T	W	R	F	S	S	M	T	W	R	F	S	S	M	T	W	R	F	S	S	M	T	W	R	F	S	S	M	T	W	R	F	S	S	M	T	W	R	F

Cycle Day	1	2	3	4	5	6	7	8	9	10	11	12	13	14	15	16	17	18	19	20	21	22	23	24	25	26	27	28	29	30	31	32	33	34	35	36	37	38	39	40
Bleeding ● ◐ ○	●	●	●	◐	○																							●												
Mucus wet / stretchy												■	■	■	■	■	■																							
Mucus damp / gooey						■		■												■			■		■															
Mucus dry / none		■	■	■			■		■	■	■							■	■		■	■		■																

Note on cycle day 6 Abigail filled in the box for "damp/gooey" because she felt damp when wiping at one bathroom visit even though she could not see or touch any mucus during the day. Similarly, on cycle day 8 she filled in the box for "damp/gooey" because she felt humid even though she could not see or touch any mucus. For cycle day 12, Abigail filled in the box for "wet/stretchy" because she felt wet during the day and when wiping even though the mucus appeared more cloudy, dense, and not stretchy.

Observing My Temperature

To measure your basal body temperature, use a digital basal body thermometer. Place the thermometer on your nightstand when you go to bed each night so you will be able to reach it in the morning without getting out of bed. One idea is to place the thermometer on top of your cell phone so you find it when you reach to turn off the alarm. When you wake up in the morning, measure your temperature before doing anything else. Try not to sit up or get out of bed and definitely do not eat or drink anything before you measure your temperature.

In the morning, place the thermometer in your mouth under your tongue. Push the tip of the thermometer probe as far under your tongue as it will go, into one of the "heat pockets" on either the left or right side of the tongue membrane in the middle of the bottom side of your tongue.

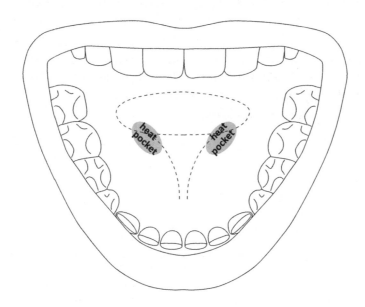

Inside bottom of mouth showing "heat pockets" at the base of the tongue

Close your mouth and turn the thermometer on. Try not to move while the thermometer is working. Do not open your mouth, talk, or let the thermometer slip while it is measuring. Try to stay awake during the measurement because if you fall back asleep, the thermometer will likely slip as your jaw muscles relax.

56

Try to measure your temperature at approximately the same time each day. Thirty minutes earlier or later is unlikely to affect the temperature [16]. Greater variations in the time you measure your temperature from day to day may cause more variability in your data and make it more difficult to see a pattern and a thermal change for some girls. Write down the time you normally measure your temperature each morning on your chart in the box labeled "Normal Time I Measure Temperature".

When the thermometer beeps that it has determined your temperature for the day, you may take the thermometer out of your mouth, set it back on your nightstand, and even go back to sleep if you'd like. Most digital thermometers remember your most recent temperature measurement so you can record it later.

Once you are up for the day, record your temperature measurement on the chart in the section labeled "Temperature" by placing a dot over the corresponding temperature. Draw a line between dots on each day to connect the dots, which will help you see patterns more easily.

If your temperature measurement is ever outside of the range shown on the chart, write in the temperature on the bottom or top line of the temperature section. If you discover your temperature is consistently below the values shown on the chart or just occasionally low, write in low values on the blank bottom line of the temperature section. For example, if you measure a temperature of 96.4°F, write in "96.4" below the last row of shown temperature values (since the lowest value shown on the chart is 96.7°F), and place a dot over it. If your temperature is ever high due to fever, being overly bundled in covers, or for fluke reasons, write in the high value on the blank top line of the temperature section. For example, if you measure a temperature of 99.8°F one day, write in "99.8" above the top row of shown temperature values (since the highest value shown on the chart is 98.5°F), and place a dot over it.

The following example shows how to record a dot over the temperature measurement and what a chart looks like when the dots are connected.

Example # 6: Recording Temperature

Abigail measures her waking basal body temperature at the same time each morning, around 6:00am, and records it on her chart once she is up for the day by placing a dot over the measured value.

		CYCLES & *Spirituality*		

Name **Abigail**   My Typical Luteal Phase Length _____   Age **16**   Year **20XX**   Chart # **1**

Date	Day of month	18	19	20	21	22	23	24	25	26	27	28	29	30	31	1	2	3	4	5	6	7	8	9	10	11	12	13	14	15	16	17	18	19	20	21	22	23	24	25	26
	Month					May																				June															
	Day of week	M	T	W	R	F	S	S	M	T	W	R	F	S	S	M	T	W	R	F	S	S	M	T	W	R	F	S	S	M	T	W	R	F	S	S	M	T	W	R	F

Temperature (°F) — Normal Time I Measure Temperature: 6:00am

Cycle Day	1	2	3	4	5	6	7	8	9	10	11	12	13	14	15	16	17	18	19	20	21	22	23	24	25	26	27	28	29	30	31	32	33	34	35	36	37	38	39	40

Observing Other Signs Unique to Me

Throughout your cycle, you may observe other signs and clues about what is going on inside your body. Note them in the section on the chart labeled "Symptoms". Physical observations may include breast tenderness, bloating, cramps, lower back aches, acne, swelling of the vulva, etc. You may also note any changes in mood including being angry, tense, tearful, sensitive, short tempered, etc. Note any signs that could possibly be related to your cycle. Over several cycles, you may begin to see trends. For example, your breast tenderness may always coincide with days of wet and slippery mucus, indicating imminent ovulation. Or your tearfulness may always occur a few days before your period, which will help you understand the hormonal contribution to your emotions.

Also use the "Symptoms" section to write down any events that may impact your cycle. These may include illness, any medications you took, or notable stress in your life. Occasionally, illness or medications can affect your temperature and/or mucus sign and may help explain if you happen to see unusual trends in a particular cycle. Stressful times in your life can also impact your cycle. When you ovulate, your body is preparing for pregnancy, the great task of carrying new life. If your body senses stress, it can sometimes react by delaying ovulation. Noting times of stress on your chart may help explain particularly long cycles.

Examples of the types of physical symptoms, moods, and life impacts you can record in the "Symptoms" section are shown below.

———————————————————— ✿ ————————————————————

Example # 7: Recording Physical Observations, Moods, and Impacts

CYCLES & Spirituality																																							
Name: Abigail	My Typical Luteal Phase Length: ___																						Age 16		Year 20XX		Chart # 1													
Cycle Day	1	2	3	4	5	6	7	8	9	10	11	12	13	14	15	16	17	18	19	20	21	22	23	24	25	26	27	28	29	30	31	32	33	34	35	36	37	38	39	40
Symptoms — physical symptoms, moods, impacts	cramps, sad	low back ache	happy	energy		stress	sleepy								joy		happy	breasts sore	brief cramps		bloated	gassy		tired		tearful	acne													

———————————————————— ✿ ————————————————————

Alyssa's story

I have had issues with bloating and flatulence for years! Public embarrassment encouraged me to talk to my doctor about it and I even saw a Gastrointestinal (GI) specialist. The GI doctor suggested the gas was most likely due to foods I ate and suggested an elimination diet. For weeks, I tried eliminating lactose, then fruit, then gassy vegetables, and then gluten. Nothing helped. About 3 months after I began charting my cycles, I noticed that my bloating and gas were correlated with ovulation and my luteal phase. What a discovery! Once I knew the real cause of the issue, I was able to use some suggestions for natural treatments to reduce the gas during those times.

Managing My Chart

Some girls find charting their cycles exciting while other girls may think writing down their mucus, temperature, and any other symptoms related to their cycle every single day sounds like a chore. If you're in the "chore" camp, consider these strategies to lessen the burden. Don't feel obligated to carry your chart with you everywhere you go. Keep it in a discreet place at home or in your bag. Start a folder of your charts so they will stay private and so you can keep all of your previous cycle charts together. Write down your observations on your chart only one time at the end of each day. Most thermometers will recall your last temperature when you turn it back on. And you can probably think back over your day to summarize the highest level of your mucus observations from the day. Writing down these two observations will not take too long. You can also use colored pens or pencils to make charting seem more fun.

Reflecting at the end of the day on your physical symptoms, mood, and any stressors or impacts may also remind you that the end of the day is often a good time for spiritual reflection or an examination of conscience regarding your day.

Becoming more aware of how you feel every day is the first step in predicting your cycles. It is also an opportunity to become more in tune with the amazing body God gave you.

Chapter 5 Summary

- To note days of bleeding on your chart, use:
    - ● for days of normal or heavy bleeding
    - ◒ for days of light bleeding
    - ○ for days of spotting

- To observe mucus:
    - Begin checking when menstrual flow lessens.
    - Become aware of the sense & feel of mucus as you go about your day and of the sight & touch of the mucus during bathroom visits.
    - Categorize the sense & feel of your mucus as either:
        - Dry
        - Damp
        - Wet
    - Categorize the see & touch of your mucus as either:
        - None
        - Gooey
        - Stretchy

- To observe temperature:
    - Use a basal body thermometer.
    - Measure your temperature as soon as you wake up each morning before getting up or drinking and at approximately the same time each day.
    - Place the thermometer deep under your tongue and keep your mouth closed.

- Note other signs and symptoms you observe that may be related to your cycles in the "Symptoms" section on your chart.

- Fill out your chart at the end of each day.
    - Consider using that time for spiritual reflection on your day.

"Entrust your works to the Lord, and your plans will succeed."
Proverbs 16:3

Chapter 6:
What My Signs Say

Now that you have started observing and recording your unique cycle signs each day, let's figure out what they are telling you! First, you'll look for mucus trends and identify the last day of wet/stretchy mucus. Then you'll look for a shift in your temperatures from a lower region to a higher region. Putting this all together, you'll be able to determine how long your luteal phase is. Recall from Chapter 3 that the luteal phase length typically remains the same for each girl from cycle to cycle. So once you know your own personal luteal phase length, you can predict your next period with amazing accuracy! We'll walk through each step with examples so you'll have plenty of practice and can apply the steps to your own charts.

Noticing My Mucus Trends
Once you have recorded your mucus on your chart you can look for a trend. A typical mucus pattern shows a few days of dry/none followed by several days of damp/gooey mucus, several days of wet/stretchy mucus, and a return to dry/none and/or damp/gooey days until the start of the next period. Notice the trend for Abigail's mucus observations in Example # 5 from Chapter 5.

Identifying My Peak Day
Looking at your mucus observations, find the last day of wet/stretchy mucus with at least three days of mucus that is "drying up" (either dry/none or damp/gooey) following it. This day will be known as "Peak Day" and will aid in determining when to expect your period. Peak Day is typically near the time of ovulation but may not always fall exactly on the day of ovulation. In the row labeled "Cycle Day", circle the cycle day corresponding to Peak Day.

The following two examples demonstrate how to find the last day of wet/stretchy mucus and circle that cycle day to denote Peak Day.

Example # 8: Identifying Peak Day

For Abigail's chart, the last day of wet/stretchy mucus is cycle day 18. Following cycle day 18, Abigail has at least three days of mucus that is either damp/gooey or dry/none. Cycle day 18 is her Peak Day so she circles that cycle day on her chart.

CYCLES & Spirituality

Name: Abigail   My Typical Luteal Phase Length _____   Age 16   Year 20XX   Chart # 1

Day of month	18	19	20	21	22	23	24	25	26	27	28	29	30	31	1	2	3	4	5	6	7	8	9	10	11	12	13	14	15	16	17	18	19	20	21	22	23	24	25	26
Month	May														June																										
Day of week	M	T	W	R	F	S	S	M	T	W	R	F	S	S	M	T	W	R	F	S	S	M	T	W	R	F	S	S	M	T	W	R	F	S	S	M	T	W	R	F

Temperature (°F) — Normal Time I Measure Temperature: 6:00am

| Cycle Day | 1 | 2 | 3 | 4 | 5 | 6 | 7 | 8 | 9 | 10 | 11 | 12 | 13 | 14 | 15 | 16 | 17 | (18) | 19 | 20 | 21 | 22 | 23 | 24 | 25 | 26 | 27 | 28 | 29 | 30 | 31 | 32 | 33 | 34 | 35 | 36 | 37 | 38 | 39 | 40 |

Bleeding: ● ◐ ○

Mucus: wet/stretchy, damp/gooey, dry/none

Symptoms, moods, impacts (physical symptoms): cramps sad, low back ache, happy, energy, stress, sleepy, joy, happy, breasts sore, bad cramps, bloated, gassy, tired, tearful, acne

Looking at Abigail's whole chart containing all of her observations and now with Peak Day circled, you may also notice other trends that correspond with the mucus trend. We will discuss them in detail soon. But first let's take a look at mucus trends for a different girl with a slightly longer cycle.

Example # 9: Identifying Peak Day

In Chloe's chart, her mucus pattern is still similar to the usual trend but she has more days of damp/gooey mucus and more days of wet/stretchy mucus prior to her Peak Day. Cycle day 23 is her last day of wet/stretchy mucus so she circles it as Peak Day.

	CYCLES & *Spirituality*

Name: **Chloe**   My Typical Luteal Phase Length _____   Age **14**   Year **20XX**   Chart # **1**

Date	Day of month	4	5	6	7	8	9	10	11	12	13	14	15	16	17	18	19	20	21	22	23	24	25	26	27	28	29	30	31	1	2	3	4	5	6	7	8	9	10	11	12
	Month														March																		April								
	Day of week	W	R	F	S	S	M	T	W	R	F	S	S	M	T	W	R	F	S	S	M	T	W	R	F	S	S	M	T	W	R	F	S	S	M	T	W	R	F	S	S

Temperature (°F) — Normal Time I Measure Temperature: 5:30am

Cycle Day	1	2	3	4	5	6	7	8	9	10	11	12	13	14	15	16	17	18	19	20	21	22	㉓	24	25	26	27	28	29	30	31	32	33	34	35	36	37	38	39	40

Bleeding: ● ◐ ○ ◐ ◐

Mucus: wet/stretchy, damp/gooey, dry/none

Symptoms: physical symptoms, moods, impacts

67

Determining My Thermal Shift

Once you have identified Peak Day, look at your temperature information to determine the thermal shift. A thermal shift typically occurs within a few days of Peak Day and can occur either before or after Peak Day. To determine the thermal shift, find three temperatures above the previous six temperatures [12] *near* Peak Day. "Near" Peak Day means the thermal shift may occur on Peak Day, a few days before Peak Day, or a few days after Peak Day. Once you have identified the three higher temperatures, circle them. You may also lightly circle the six lower temperatures as you count back.

The following two examples show how to find the three temperatures higher than the previous six on Abigail and Chloe's charts.

Example # 10: Determining Thermal Shift

In Abigail's chart, the temperatures on cycle days 18, 19, and 20 are near Peak Day and are above the previous six temperatures on cycle days 12-17. She circles them on her chart.

CYCLES & *Spirituality*

Name	Abigail	My Typical Luteal Phase Length		Age	16	Year	20XX	Chart #	1

Day of month	18	19	20	21	22	23	24	25	26	27	28	29	30	31	1	2	3	4	5	6	7	8	9	10	11	12	13	14	15	16	17	18	19	20	21	22	23	24	25	26
Month							May																							June										
Day of week	M	T	W	R	F	S	S	M	T	W	R	F	S	S	M	T	W	R	F	S	S	M	T	W	R	F	S	S	M	T	W	R	F	S	S	M	T	W	R	F

Temperature (°F) — Normal Time I Measure Temperature: 6:00am

Cycle Day	1	2	3	4	5	6	7	8	9	10	11	12	13	14	15	16	17	(18)	19	20	21	22	23	24	25	26	27	28	29	30	31	32	33	34	35	36	37	38	39	40

Bleeding ● ◗ ○

Mucus: wet / stretchy, damp / gooey, dry / none

Symptoms, moods, impacts: cramps, sad | low back ache | happy | energy | stress | sleepy | joy | happy | breasts sore | brief cramps | bloated | gassy | tired | tearful | acne

Some girls find it helpful to lay a straight and thin object, like a pencil or piece of string, horizontally across the chart as a visual aid. Adjust the location of the straight object until you find six temperatures below the object and three temperatures above the object. Try this technique in the next example.

Example # 11: Determining Thermal Shift

Chloe places a straight pencil across her chart and adjusts it until she finds three temperatures above the pencil and three temperatures below the pencil. In Chloe's chart, the temperatures on cycle days 24, 25, and 26 are near Peak Day and are above the pencil while the previous six temperatures on cycle days 18-23 are below the pencil.

CYCLES & Spirituality

Name: Chloe My Typical Luteal Phase Length _____ Age 14 Year 20XX Chart # 1

Day of month	4	5	6	7	8	9	10	11	12	13	14	15	16	17	18	19	20	21	22	23	24	25	26	27	28	29	30	31	1	2	3	4	5	6	7	8	9	10	11	12
Month													March																					April						
Day of week	W	R	F	S	S	M	T	W	R	F	S	S	M	T	W	R	F	S	S	M	T	W	R	F	S	S	M	T	W	R	F	S	S	M	T	W	R	F	S	S

Temperature (°F) — Normal Time I Measure Temperature: 5:30am

| Cycle Day | 1 | 2 | 3 | 4 | 5 | 6 | 7 | 8 | 9 | 10 | 11 | 12 | 13 | 14 | 15 | 16 | 17 | 18 | 19 | 20 | 21 | 22 | 23 | 24 | 25 | 26 | 27 | 28 | 29 | 30 | 31 | 32 | 33 | 34 | 35 | 36 | 37 | 38 | 39 | 40 |
| Bleeding ● ○ | | | | | | | | | | | | | | | | | | | | | | | | | | | | | | | | | | | | | | | | |

Mucus: wet / stretchy, damp / gooey, dry / none

Symptoms: physical symptoms, moods, impacts

For some girls, the thermal shift may occur very sharply with a large rise in temperature but for other girls, the thermal shift may occur more gradually (like stair steps) over a few days. Temperatures in the thermal shift are typically at least 0.4°F above the six temperatures prior to the thermal shift.

70

To label the thermal shift, draw a horizontal line through the highest temperature in the previous six. This will be your Thermal Shift Line. For *Cycles & Spirituality*, drawing the Thermal Shift Line is a visual aid to help you interpret your chart and determine the length of your luteal phase.

The next two examples show how to draw the Thermal Shift Line in Abigail and Chloe's charts.

Example # 12: Drawing the Thermal Shift Line

In Abigail's chart, the highest temperature of the previous six temperatures is 97.6°F so she draws a horizontal line through 97.6°F. This is her Thermal Shift Line for this cycle.

CYCLES & Spirituality

Name: Abigail   My Typical Luteal Phase Length _____   Age 16   Year 20XX   Chart # 1

Day of month	18	19	20	21	22	23	24	25	26	27	28	29	30	31	1	2	3	4	5	6	7	8	9	10	11	12	13	14	15	16	17	18	19	20	21	22	23	24	25	26
Month					May																		June																	
Day of week	M	T	W	R	F	S	S	M	T	W	R	F	S	S	M	T	W	R	F	S	S	M	T	W	R	F	S	S	M	T	W	R	F	S	S	M	T	W	R	F

| Cycle Day | 1 | 2 | 3 | 4 | 5 | 6 | 7 | 8 | 9 | 10 | 11 | 12 | 13 | 14 | 15 | 16 | 17 | 18 | 19 | 20 | 21 | 22 | 23 | 24 | 25 | 26 | 27 | 28 | 29 | 30 | 31 | 32 | 33 | 34 | 35 | 36 | 37 | 38 | 39 | 40 |

71

Example # 13: Drawing the Thermal Shift Line

In Chloe's chart, the highest temperature of the previous six temperatures is 97.5°F so she draws the Thermal Shift Line at 97.5°F for this cycle.

CYCLES & Spirituality																																									

Name: **Chloe**   My Typical Luteal Phase Length _____   Age **14**   Year **20XX**   Chart # **1**

Date	Day of month	4	5	6	7	8	9	10	11	12	13	14	15	16	17	18	19	20	21	22	23	24	25	26	27	28	29	30	31	1	2	3	4	5	6	7	8	9	10	11	12
	Month												March																						April							
	Day of week	W	R	F	S	S	M	T	W	R	F	S	S	M	T	W	R	F	S	S	M	T	W	R	F	S	S	M	T	W	R	F	S	S	M	T	W	R	F	S	S

Normal Time I Measure Temperature: 5:30am

Cycle Day	1	2	3	4	5	6	7	8	9	10	11	12	13	14	15	16	17	18	19	20	21	22	23	24	25	26	27	28	29	30	31	32	33	34	35	36	37	38	39	40

| Bleeding ● ◐ ○ | ● | ● | ◐ | ◐ | | | | | | | | | | | | | | | | | | | | | | | | | | | | | | | ● | | | | | |

Mucus	wet / stretchy																																									
	damp / gooey																																									
	dry / none																																									

Symptoms	physical																																									
	symptoms,																																									
	moods,																																									
	impacts																																									

The thermal shift, in combination with the mucus Peak Day, gives you a general idea of the time of ovulation each cycle. The exact moment or day of ovulation may not correspond exactly with Peak Day or the first day of your thermal shift but are indicators of how your hormones are changing, likely indicating that ovulation is imminent, occurring, or has just occurred.

Also notice that Peak Day and the thermal shift can only be determined in retrospect (after they occur). Mucus dries up and your waking temperature rises in response to an increase in production of the hormone progesterone, which is produced after ovulation. This means that charting does not verify ovulation until after you have ovulated. But becoming aware of your body and cycle signs can give you clues each cycle about what is occurring inside your body. Taking a look at the big picture on your chart – noticing your mucus trends, your temperature range and patterns, and your overall symptoms – will help indicate when your hormones may be preparing to make changes. Then you can begin to notice how those hormonal changes impact your feelings or other aspects of your life.

Katherine's story

I was skeptical of charting my cycles. I am an ultrasound technologist so I have a background in the medical field. Charting cycles is not taught in the healthcare industry and is even looked down upon as inaccurate. But I decided it couldn't hurt to give it a try and was actually able to correlate my chart with what I saw on ultrasound when I looked at my own body! Most medical books assume ovulation occurs on day 14 of a cycle but I could see by my chart that I had probably not yet ovulated and, sure enough, ultrasound revealed that my ovaries had not yet released an egg that cycle. When my chart showed a sustained thermal shift, ultrasound confirmed that an egg had released. As I continued to chart several cycles, I became more confident in the science behind my observable signs. Then, unexpectedly, I discovered that learning to chart my cycles led me to learn God's plan for my body and for marriage. I saw it was so beautiful and wanted to learn more about God's design and plan for all things.

Determining My Luteal Phase

Once you have identified Peak Day with your cervical mucus drying up afterward and you can visually identify the shift in temperatures to a higher level, you are in the luteal phase of your cycle. The luteal phase of the cycle is the most repeatable phase for each girl. Even if your overall cycles are very irregular in length, the luteal phase will still be relatively constant each cycle! This amazing design is what will predict when your period will start.

To determine your luteal phase length, count the number of days after the thermal shift but prior to the start of your next period (in other words, begin counting with the first day that your temperature is above the Thermal Shift Line and end counting the day before your next period).

Write this number in the section labeled "My Typical Luteal Phase Length" on your next chart for your next cycle.

The following two examples demonstrate how to determine the length of the luteal phase.

Example # 14: Determining Luteal Phase

In Abigail's chart #1, her luteal phase begins on cycle day 18, the first day her temperature is above the Thermal Shift Line. Notice that Abigail begins her next period on cycle day 28 (June 14) so this day does not count as part of her luteal phase. Her luteal phase lasts from cycle day 18 to cycle day 27 for a total of 10 days. On June 14, Abigail will start a new chart and label it chart #2. On the line labeled "My Typical Luteal Phase Length" on chart #2, she will write __10__ days.

CYCLES & Spirituality

Name __Abigail__   My Typical Luteal Phase Length ____   Age __16__   Year __20XX__   Chart # __1__

Date	Day of month	18	19	20	21	22	23	24	25	26	27	28	29	30	31	1	2	3	4	5	6	7	8	9	10	11	12	13	14	15	16	17	18	19	20	21	22	23	24	25	26
	Month					May																			June																
	Day of week	M	T	W	R	F	S	S	M	T	W	R	F	S	S	M	T	W	R	F	S	S	M	T	W	R	F	S	S	M	T	W	R	F	S	S	M	T	W	R	F

Temperature (°F) — Normal Time I Measure Temperature: 6:00am

| Cycle Day | 1 | 2 | 3 | 4 | 5 | 6 | 7 | 8 | 9 | 10 | 11 | 12 | 13 | 14 | 15 | 16 | 17 | (18) | 19 | 20 | 21 | 22 | 23 | 24 | 25 | 26 | 27 | 28 | 29 | 30 | 31 | 32 | 33 | 34 | 35 | 36 | 37 | 38 | 39 | 40 |

Bleeding ● ◑ ○

Mucus	wet / stretchy
	damp / gooey
	dry / none

Symptoms	physical symptoms, moods, impacts

Symptom notations: cramps, sad · low back ache · happy · energy · stress · sleepy · joy · happy · breasts sore · brief cramps · bloated · gassy · tired · tearful · acne

Example # 15: Determining Luteal Phase

In Chloe's chart #1, her luteal phase begins on cycle day 24, the first day of temperatures above the Thermal Shift Line. Notice that cycle day 35 (April 7) does not count as part of her luteal phase because she started her next period this day. Her luteal phase lasts from cycle day 24 to cycle day 34 for a luteal phase length of 11 days. On April 7, Chloe will start chart #2. On the line labeled "My Typical Luteal Phase Length" on chart #2, she will write 11 days.

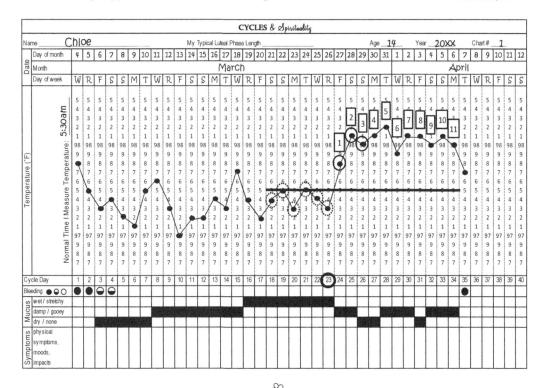

If you have identified a thermal shift from low temperatures to high temperatures and then your temperature happens to dip down below the Thermal Shift Line but comes back up, you should still count the lower temperature day(s) as part of your luteal phase.

Your luteal phase length should stay about the same each cycle but may vary slightly (usually +/- 1 day). Be sure to determine your luteal phase length for each chart to find your own normal variability. You can write a range in the line labeled "My Typical Luteal Phase Length", such as "11-13 days". Also be aware that your typical luteal phase length may get longer as you get older. For example, you may observe luteal phase lengths of 9-11 days for the first year you chart your cycles but then may start to observe luteal phase lengths of 12-14 days in your later teen or young adult years.

Now, let's put everything together to practice determining luteal phase length step-by-step. In the following practice chart, use Emily's daily observations for cervical mucus and basal body temperature to interpret her chart and determine her luteal phase length. Use these steps:
1) Identify Peak Day as the last day of wet/stretchy mucus followed by at least three days of mucus that is "drying up".
2) Determine the thermal shift by finding three temperatures higher than the previous six temperatures near Peak Day.
3) Draw the Thermal Shift Line through the highest of the six temperatures in the previous six.
4) Determine the luteal phase length by counting the number of days after the thermal shift but prior to the start of the next period (begin counting with the first day that temperature is above the Thermal Shift Line and end counting the day before the next period).

Practice Chart # 1

What is Emily's luteal phase length this cycle?

CYCLES & *Spirituality*

| Name | Emily | | | | My Typical Luteal Phase Length | 11-12 days | | | | | | | | Age | 15 | | Year | 20XX | | | Chart # | 7 | |

Date	Day of month	27	27	28	29	30	1	2	3	4	5	6	7	8	9	10	11	12	13	14	15	16	17	18	19	20	21	22	23	24	25	26	27	28	29	30	31	1	2	3	4
	Month	September														October																							November			
	Day of week	S	M	T	W	R	F	S	S	M	T	W	R	F	S	S	M	T	W	R	F	S	S	M	T	W	R	F	S	S	M	T	W	R	F	S	S	M	T	W	R

Temperature (°F) — Normal Time I Measure Temperature: 5:30am

| Cycle Day | 1 | 2 | 3 | 4 | 5 | 6 | 7 | 8 | 9 | 10 | 11 | 12 | 13 | 14 | 15 | 16 | 17 | 18 | 19 | 20 | 21 | 22 | 23 | 24 | 25 | 26 | 27 | 28 | 29 | 30 | 31 | 32 | 33 | 34 | 35 | 36 | 37 | 38 | 39 | 40 |

Bleeding ● ◐ ○

Mucus	wet / stretchy
	damp / gooey
	dry / none

| Symptoms | physical symptoms, moods, impacts |

[See the Answer and interpretation of Practice Chart #1 in Appendix B.]

79

Starting a New Chart

On the first day of your next menstruation, mark any bleeding on your chart in the row labeled "Bleeding". Then begin a new chart and also mark the first day of bleeding in the row labeled "Bleeding" for cycle day 1 of the new chart. Transfer the temperature measurement to cycle day 1 on the new chart, as well. This means that the last day you make observations on one chart will be the same day you start a new chart with cycle day 1. The information you record in these two spaces on separate charts will be identical since they are the same day.

Technically, this first day of bleeding is cycle day 1 of the next cycle. But recording this as a day of bleeding on the previous chart can help you keep track and remember that the previous cycle ended with a menstruation. Recording the information twice is simply a way of tying one chart to the next.

For Abigail's chart in Example #14, her cycle day 28 on her first chart will become her cycle day 1 on her second chart. She will transfer the exact same information from cycle day 28 on chart #1 to her new chart #2. She will mark a ● for normal to heavy bleeding on cycle day 1 in the line for "Bleeding" and mark the temperature on cycle day 1 at 97.8°F.

For Chloe's chart in Example #15, her cycle day 35 on her first chart will become her cycle day 1 on her second chart. She will mark a ● for normal to heavy bleeding on cycle day 1 in the line for "Bleeding" and mark the temperature on cycle day 1 at 97.7°F.

Sometime around the start of your period, your temperature will drop back to its pre-ovulation levels. This can occur a day or two before your period starts, on the day your period starts, or a few days after your period starts. Your temperature may drop gradually (a few tenths of a degree each day) or all at once. Over several cycles, you will learn what is normal for your own body.

My Cycle Length

The length of your cycle is the number of days from the first day of your period to the day before the first day of your next period.

For Abigail's chart #1 in Example #14, her cycle length is 27 days. For Chloe's chart #1 in Example #15, her cycle length is 34 days.

Predicting My Period

Once you have determined your own luteal phase length by charting your own cycles, it should stay about the same each cycle, give or take a day. A typical luteal phase length is 10-14 days. (Luteal phases may be shorter for some girls in the first year of ovulatory cycles [17].) For example, if your typical luteal phase is 13 days, you will know to expect your period 12-14 days after your thermal shift has occurred in future cycles.

To predict your next period, first look back at your luteal phase lengths for your past several cycles and write the range in the box labeled "My Typical Luteal Phase Length" at the top of your next chart. As you record your mucus and temperature observations each day, notice the trends. When you have enough information to identify Peak Day and a thermal shift, label them on your chart. Begin counting the number of days in your luteal phase with the first day that your temperature is above the Thermal Shift Line. Count days until you reach the number of days in your "My Typical Luteal Phase Length". For example, if your typical luteal phase length is 13 days, count 13 days from the first day of your thermal shift. Around this day is when you should expect your next period.

The following are two examples of how Abigail and Chloe can predict when their next period will arrive based on the information they learned from their very first cycle charting.

Example # 16: Predicting My Period

With Abigail's second cycle of charting, she can predict when her next period will arrive. Her chart #2 is below. On what day should she expect to start her period this cycle?

CYCLES & Spirituality

Name: **Abigail**   My Typical Luteal Phase Length: **10 days**   Age: **16**   Year: **20XX**   Chart #: **2**

Date	Day of month	14	15	16	17	18	19	20	21	22	23	24	25	26	27	28	29	30	1	2	3	4	5	6	7	8	9	10	11	12	13	14	15	16	17	18	19	20	21	22	23
	Month							June																			July													
	Day of week	S	M	T	W	R	F	S	S	M	T	W	R	F	S	S	M	T	W	R	F	S	S	M	T	W	R	F	S	S	M	T	W	R	F	S	S	M	T	W	R	F

Temperature (°F) — Normal Time I Measure Temperature: **6:00am**

Cycle Day	1	2	3	4	5	6	7	8	9	10	11	12	13	14	15	16	17	18	19	20	21	22	23	24	25	26	27	28	29	30	31	32	33	34	35	36	37	38	39	40

Abigail is currently on cycle day 18 of chart #2. Based on her mucus observations, she has identified Peak Day as cycle day 15. She determined her thermal shift by finding three temperatures higher than the previous six near Peak Day and drew the Thermal Shift Line on her chart. She knows her luteal phase length last cycle was 10 days.

82

Based on this information, Abigail can count 10 days from the first day of her luteal phase (first day of temperatures above the Thermal Shift Line). This estimates that her luteal phase this cycle will last from cycle day 16 to around cycle day 25, meaning she should expect her next period to start around cycle day 26 (July 9).

Since luteal phase length can vary just slightly and Abigail only has one previous cycle history for observing her luteal phase length, she should be prepared for her period to start somewhere between cycle days 25-27.

Example # 17: Predicting My Period

With Chloe's second cycle of charting, we can predict when her next period will arrive.

CYCLES & Spirituality

Name **Chloe**   My Typical Luteal Phase Length **11 days**   Age **14**   Year **20XX**   Chart # **2**

Date																																								
Day of month	7	8	9	10	11	12	13	14	15	16	17	18	19	20	21	22	23	24	25	26	27	28	29	30	1	2	3	4	5	6	7	8	9	10	11	12	13	14	15	16
Month											April																						May							
Day of week	T	W	R	F	S	S	M	T	W	R	F	S	S	M	T	W	R	F	S	S	M	T	W	R	F	S	S	M	T	W	R	F	S	S	M	T	W	R	F	S

Temperature (°F) — Normal Time I Measure Temperature: 5:30am

Cycle Day	1	2	3	4	5	6	7	8	9	10	11	12	13	14	15	16	17	18	19	20	21	22	23	24	25	26	27	28	29	30	31	32	33	34	35	36	37	38	39	40

Bleeding ● ● ○

Mucus: wet / stretchy, damp / gooey, dry / none

Symptoms: physical symptoms, moods, impacts

Chloe is currently on cycle day 30 of chart #2. Based on her mucus observations, she has identified Peak Day as cycle day 26. She determined her thermal shift by finding three temperatures higher than the previous six near Peak Day and drew the Thermal Shift Line on her chart. She knows her luteal phase length last cycle was 11 days.

Based on this information, Chloe can count 11 days from the first day of her luteal phase to estimate that her luteal phase this cycle will last from cycle day 28 to around cycle day 38, meaning she should expect her next period to start around cycle day 39 (May 15).

Since luteal phase length can vary just slightly and Chloe only has one previous cycle history for observing her luteal phase length, she should be prepared for her period to start somewhere between cycle days 38-40.

⸻ ✿ ⸻

Interpreting My Whole Chart

Ready to put it all together? Here is a summary of the steps to interpret your whole chart and predict when your period will arrive:

1) Identify Peak Day as the last day of wet/stretchy mucus followed by at least three days of mucus that is "drying up".
2) Determine the thermal shift by finding three temperatures higher than the previous six temperatures near Peak Day.
3) Draw the Thermal Shift Line through the highest of the six temperatures in the previous six.
4) Look at your Typical Luteal Phase length from your previous cycles and apply it to your current chart. Start counting with the first day of temperatures above the Thermal Shift Line on your current cycle.
5) Predict your period will arrive the day after your Typical Luteal Phase length.

In the following practice charts, use Emily and Madison's daily observations for cervical mucus and basal body temperature to interpret their charts and predict when their next period will arrive. Use the steps above.

Practice Chart # 2

When should Emily expect her period to start this cycle?

CYCLES & Spirituality																																							

Name: **Emily** My Typical Luteal Phase Length **11-12 days** Age **15** Year **20XX** Chart # **8**

Date	Day of month	4	5	6	7	8	9	10	11	12	13	14	15	16	17	18	19	20	21	22	23	24	25	26	27	28	29	30	1	2	3	4	5	6	7	8	9	10	11	12	13
	Month										November																							December							
	Day of week	R	F	S	S	M	T	W	R	F	S	S	M	T	W	R	F	S	S	M	T	W	R	F	S	S	M	T	W	R	F	S	S	M	T	W	R	F	S	S	M

Temperature (°F) — Normal Time I Measure Temperature: 5:30am

Cycle Day	1	2	3	4	5	6	7	8	9	10	11	12	13	14	15	16	17	18	19	20	21	22	23	24	25	26	27	28	29	30	31	32	33	34	35	36	37	38	39	40
Bleeding ●◐○	◐	●	●	●	◐	◐																																		

Mucus:
- wet / stretchy
- damp / gooey
- dry / none

Symptoms: physical symptoms, moods, impacts

[See Answer to Practice Chart #2 in Appendix B.]

Practice Chart # 3

When will Madison's period start this cycle?

CYCLES & *Spirituality*																																							

Name **Madison** My Typical Luteal Phase Length **13-14 days** Age **19** Year **20XX** Chart # **13**

Date	Day of month	1	2	3	4	5	6	7	8	9	10	11	12	13	14	15	16	17	18	19	20	21	22	23	24	25	26	27	28	29	30
	Month	November																													
	Day of week	S	M	T	W	R	F	S	S	M	T	W	R	F	S	S	M	T	W	R	F	S	S	M	T	W	R	F	S	S	M

Temperature (°F) — Normal Time I Measure Temperature: **7:00am**

(temperature graph plotted across days)

Cycle Day	1	2	3	4	5	6	7	8	9	10	11	12	13	14	15	16	17	18	19	20	21	22	23	24	25	26	27	28	29	30	31	32	33	34	35	36	37	38	39	40
Bleeding ● ◐ ○	●	●	●	◐	◐																																			

Mucus
| wet / stretchy |
| damp / gooey |
| dry / none |

Symptoms (physical symptoms, moods, impacts): sad & bloated; emotional & crampy; fatigued; not enough sleep; happy; bloated; moody & gassy

[See Answer to Practice Chart #3 in Appendix B.]

88

Breakthrough Bleeding
If you experience bleeding without seeing a sustained thermal shift previously in that cycle, mark the bleeding on the current chart and do not start a new chart. Bleeding that is not preceded by a thermal shift is not a true menstruation and is called breakthrough bleeding.

In young women, it is common in the early years following puberty for cycles to be irregular while the reproductive system is developing. During this time, the brain may release FSH to prepare an egg and the reproductive organs may produce some estrogen but the body may not actually ovulate. As estrogen is produced, the lining of the uterus may build up to a point where it cannot sustain itself and breakthrough bleeding can occur [24]. These anovulatory cycles may occur for the first few years following menarche and are considered normal [17, 19]. Charting during anovulatory cycles may reveal basal body temperatures that seem erratic and do not exhibit regions of low and high temperatures or a thermal shift.

After a girl's body establishes more regular ovulatory cycles, occasional breakthrough bleeding can still be normal, especially in long cycles. Some girls experience light bleeding or spotting around the time of ovulation. If breakthrough bleeding occurs on a regular basis, it may be a sign of other health concerns and you should talk to your doctor.

Eva's chart shows an example of breakthrough bleeding in a long cycle.

Example # 18: Breakthrough Bleeding in a Long Ovulatory Cycle

CYCLES & *Spirituality*

Name ___Eva___ My Typical Luteal Phase Length __9-10 days__ Age __16__ Year __20XX__ Chart # __10__

Day of month	13	14	15	16	17	18	19	20	21	22	23	24	25	26	27	28	29	30	31	1	2	3	4	5	6	7	8	9	10	11	12	13	14	15	16	17	18	19	20	21
Month						August																						September												
Day of week	R	F	S	S	M	T	W	R	F	S	S	M	T	W	R	F	S	S	M	T	W	R	F	S	S	M	T	W	R	F	S	S	M	T	W	R	F	S	S	M	T

(Temperature (°F) grid — Normal Time I Measure Temperature: 6:30am)

| Cycle Day | 1 | 2 | 3 | 4 | 5 | 6 | 7 | 8 | 9 | 10 | 11 | 12 | 13 | 14 | 15 | 16 | 17 | 18 | 19 | 20 | 21 | 22 | 23 | 24 | 25 | 26 | 27 | 28 | 29 | 30 | 31 | 32 | 33 | 34 | 35 | 36 | 37 | 38 | 39 | 40 |

Bleeding: ● ○ ○ ● ● ● ● ○ (days 27–29) ○ ○ ○ (day 40) ○

Mucus: wet/stretchy; damp/gooey; dry/none

Symptoms, moods, impacts: 1st day of school; full of energy; happy; mild cramp

On cycle days 16-19, Eva's mucus was wet/stretchy. However, since she did not observe a temperature shift around these days, she knows cycle day 19 was not a true Peak Day and the bleeding she observed on cycle days 27-29 was not a true menstruation because it did not follow ovulation. Eva's second patch of wet/stretchy mucus on cycle days 25-30 was followed by a thermal shift so she knows cycle day 30 was a true Peak Day. The bleeding that began on cycle day 40 coincided with her typical luteal phase length and was a true menstruation. Without charting, Eva would likely have thought the bleeding on cycle days 27-29 was a "light period". She probably would not have been expecting to bleed again less than two weeks later and might have been caught off guard. Since she was charting, she knows that the bleeding on cycle days 27-29 was breakthrough bleeding and was prepared for her period.

Missed Temperatures

If you miss a day or two of measuring your temperature or if the temperature you measure seems abnormal for some reason, you may still be able to accurately predict when your period will arrive. If you miss measuring your temperature, do not record a temperature on your chart that day. If the temperature you measure seems abnormal, record the temperature but place an "X" over the dot to indicate it might be inaccurate. If the days of missed temperatures are not in the thermal shift or the six days prior to the thermal shift, your assessment of the thermal shift and the luteal phase will not be affected. If the missed temperatures are in the thermal shift or the six days prior to the thermal shift, use Peak Day and the temperature measurements you do have to approximate when your luteal phase began.

If it is unclear if the missing temperature(s) would fall in the six days prior (lower region) or the thermal shift (higher region), calculate the day of your next period using both possibilities and know your period could begin anytime in that range.

Olivia's chart shows an example of how to estimate when her period will begin even though she missed measuring her temperature some days.

Example # 19: Missed Temperature near Peak Day

		CYCLES & *Spirituality*					
Name **Olivia**	My Typical Luteal Phase Length **14 days**	Age **17**	Year **20XX**	Chart # **5**			

	Day of month	24	25	26	27	28	29	30	31	1	2	3	4	5	6	7	8	9	10	11	12	13	14	15	16	17	18	19	20	21	22	23	24	25	26	27	28	29	30
Date	Month			October																November																			
	Day of week	S	S	M	T	W	R	F	S	S	M	T	W	R	F	S	S	M	T	W	R	F	S	S	M	T	W	R	F	S	S	M	T	W	R	F	S	S	M

Temperature (°F) — Normal Time I Measure Temperature: 5:45am

Cycle Day	1	2	3	4	5	6	7	8	9	10	11	12	13	(14)	15	16	17	18	19	20	21	22	23	24	25	26	27	28	29	30	31	32	33	34	35	36	37	38	39	40
Bleeding	●	●	○	●	●	●	○	○	○																															

Mucus: wet / stretchy; damp / gooey; dry / none

Symptoms: physical symptoms, moods, impacts — "slept in", "forgot temp"

In Olivia's chart, the missed temperature on cycle day 8 turned out not to impact her chart interpretation. The missed temperature on cycle day 15 is near Peak Day and falls directly in between the thermal shift making the interpretation slightly more vague. She cannot know for sure if her thermal shift began on cycle day 15 or cycle day 16. Since she knows her luteal phase is typically 14 days, she can estimate that her period should start around cycle day 29 or 30 and should not be surprised if it starts anywhere between cycle day 28 and 31 (due to the normal slight variation in luteal phase length combined with the uncertainty of the start day of her luteal phase this cycle). The missed temperature on cycle day 22 does not impact her chart interpretation.

Chapter 6 Summary

- Noticing trends in your cervical mucus and basal body temperature will help you interpret your chart and predict when your period will arrive.

- To identify Peak Day:
    - Find the last day of wet/stretchy mucus followed by at least three days of mucus that is "drying up" (i.e. not wet/stretchy).
    - Circle Peak Day in the "Cycle Day" line on your chart.

- To determine the thermal shift:
    - Find three temperatures higher than the previous six temperatures near Peak Day.
        - Use a straight line object to help you visually see the shift.
    - Circle the temperatures to visually help your interpretation.

- To draw the Thermal Shift Line:
    - Find the highest of the six temperatures you circled that are below your straight line object.
    - Draw a horizontal line through that temperature.

- To determine your luteal phase length:
    - Count the number of days that your temperature is above the Thermal Shift Line prior to the start of your next period.
        - Your luteal phase length will be relatively constant from cycle to cycle.
    - Write your typical luteal phase length on your next chart in the top line labeled "My Typical Luteal Phase Length".

- To predict when your period will arrive (starting with chart #2):
    - Use your typical luteal phase length from your previous cycle(s).
    - Number the days starting with the first day your temperature is above your Thermal Shift Line for your current cycle.
    - Predict your period will arrive the day after your typical luteal phase length.

- Bleeding not preceded by a thermal shift is called "breakthrough bleeding" and is not a true menstruation.

Part III:
Living Naturally with the Body God Gave Me

Now that you can observe your signs, know when you've ovulated, and predict when your period will start, how does that help you deal with all the other issues that come with menstrual cycles? Simply charting your signs doesn't stop cramps or the emotional roller coaster of hormones, but understanding the changes going on in your body on any given day can help you identify the cause of certain symptoms. Chapter 7 discusses how life events like stress, illness, and medications can impact your cycle and your chart. Chapter 8 identifies the many real symptoms associated with your menstrual cycle and offers realistic, practical, and natural ways to handle these symptoms. Finally, Chapter 9 examines artificial means of "regulating your cycle" using birth control, assesses how these artificial hormones interfere with your body's natural chemistry, and presents the side effects of birth control pills. By the time you reach Chapter 9, perhaps you'll find that using birth control as a means of predicting your cycles is simply not necessary with the knowledge of cycle awareness.

"Consider it all joy, my brothers, when you encounter various trials, for you know that the testing of your faith produces perseverance. And let perseverance be perfect, so that you may be perfect and complete, lacking in nothing."

James 1:2-4

Chapter 7:
Impacts to My Cycle and Signs

Some external factors can impact the timing of ovulation or the normal signs your body displays throughout your cycle.

Stress

Stress can come from many events in our lives including school exams, dating, college applications or job interviews, surgery, planning a wedding, a death in the family, or even smaller events that seem stressful to you. Most of us recognize stress as a cause of high blood pressure, headaches, or difficulty sleeping. But stress can also have an impact on your menstrual cycle. Depending where you are in your cycle when the stressful event occurs, your body may be impacted differently.

Before ovulation

If you are in the first half of your cycle, prior to ovulation, when you experience a stressful event, your body may react by delaying ovulation. You can think of this as your body's subconscious motherly instinct to protect a potential new life. In the first half of your cycle, your body is preparing for a potential pregnancy. If a stressful event occurs, your body may say "Whoa! I'm not prepared to handle this stress PLUS a new baby" and send signals to delay the release of an egg until your body is back to a more steady state.

If stress is causing a delay in ovulation, you may see an extended number of days of damp/gooey mucus or wet/stretchy mucus compared to your usual. Alternatively, you may experience wet/stretchy mucus followed by a time of drying up (a return to damp/gooey or dry/none mucus). This pattern will give the impression of a Peak Day but will not be accompanied by a thermal shift. The body will then usually return to wet/stretchy mucus and you will be able to identify a true Peak Day with a corresponding thermal shift. For events that seem to have longer-lasting stress, your body may respond by avoiding ovulation and producing an anovulatory cycle with eventual breakthrough bleeding (bleeding that was never preceded by ovulation as indicated by a thermal shift).

Lexi's chart shows the impact of stress on her cycle during her final exam week.

-- ✿ --

Example # 20: Impact of Stress on Cycle Prior to Ovulation

CYCLES & *Spirituality*

Name ___Lexi___   My Typical Luteal Phase Length ___13 days___   Age __20__   Year __20XX-XX__   Chart # ___19___

Date	Day of month	27	28	29	30	1	2	3	4	5	6	7	8	9	10	11	12	13	14	15	16	17	18	19	20	21	22	23	24	25	26	27	28	29	30	31	1	2	3	4	5	6	7
	Month	November														December																					January						
	Day of week	F	S	S	M	T	W	R	F	S	S	M	T	W	R	F	S	S	M	T	W	R	F	S	S	M	T	W	R	F	S	S	M	T	W	R	F	S	S	M	T	W	R

(Temperature chart, measured at 7:00am)

Cycle Day	1	2	3	4	5	6	7	8	9	10	11	12	13	14	15	16	17	18	19	20	21	22	23	24	25	26	**27**	28	29	30	31	32	33	34	35	36	37	38	39	40	41	42

Bleeding ●●○

Mucus: wet/stretchy, damp/gooey, dry/none

Symptoms, moods, impacts: Final Exam Week Stress; mild cramps; back ache, cramps

Lexi had an extended number of days of wet/stretchy mucus on cycle days 12-19. It appeared her body was preparing for ovulation. However, the stress of studying for her final exam week seemed to impact her cycle around cycle day 19. She had several days of mucus that alternated between damp/gooey and wet/stretchy before another shorter patch of wet/stretchy mucus on cycle days 24-27. This patch of wet/stretchy mucus culminates with a Peak Day on cycle day 27 since there is a corresponding thermal shift beginning on cycle day 29. Based on her typical luteal phase of 13 days, Lexi knew to expect her period around cycle days 41-43.

-- ✿ --

For some girls, delayed ovulation may occur at the smallest sense of stress. For other girls with extremely consistent cycles, even very stressful events may not impact their cycle enough to delay ovulation. Just keep in mind that every girl, and every cycle, can be different and you'll be able to observe if or when stress is impacting your cycle.

After ovulation

If you are in the second half of your cycle (the luteal phase after ovulation) and you experience a stressful event, the timing of your period should not be affected. The luteal phase of your cycle, which is typically consistent for each individual girl, will remain the same, regardless of stress. However, you may notice an increase in premenstrual symptoms or a change in your ability to handle them. During stressful events, your normal fatigue, cramps, and emotional symptoms during the days leading up to menstruation may seem significantly worse than usual. Awareness is the first step in dealing with these symptoms. The next chapter discusses other specific strategies for the physical and emotional symptoms associated with your cycle.

Body Weight & Body Fat

Having a non-healthy body weight, or a non-healthy percentage of body fat, can cause menstrual cycle irregularities and/or worsen menstrual symptoms. A non-healthy body weight can be either overweight OR underweight. Likewise for body fat, having too much OR not enough body fat can impact your cycle.

A common measure of healthy body weight is the Body Mass Index (BMI), which is based on your height and weight and can be calculated or determined from BMI Tables found on the internet [25]. The National Institutes of Health uses the following categories for BMI ranges [26]:

Underweight: < 18.5
Normal weight: 18.5-24.9
Overweight: 25-29.9
Obesity: ≥ 30

Percentage body fat can be calculated using body fat calipers, bioelectric impedance, or hydrostatic weighing (which involves submersion of your entire body in a tank of water), all rather impractical for an individual to perform alone. However, evaluating the image of your own body objectively relative to your lifestyle and known BMI can give you an idea of your body fat range. If your

BMI reports you are of normal weight but your body is extremely slender and you eat a low fat or low calorie diet, there is a reasonable likelihood you may have a low percentage of body fat. If your BMI reports you are overweight but your body appears muscular and you are extremely active in sports, your percentage body fat may be normal. Ask your doctor about a healthy BMI and percentage body fat for your own unique body.

Your cycle chart may also give you clues about your percentage body fat.

Being Overweight

Being overweight or having a high percentage of body fat may cause short luteal phases, poor mucus patterns, poor temperature rises, or amenorrhea (the absence or cessation of ovulation & menstruation). Being overweight or having a high percentage of body fat can contribute to excess levels of estrogen in your body, which can increase weight gain, worsen PMS symptoms, and increase your risk of uterine fibroid tumors and breast cancer [27]. Obtaining an appropriate body weight and percentage of body fat can improve menstrual cycle function.

Being Underweight

Using the BMI table can determine if you are underweight for your height. However, even girls of a healthy weight may not have enough body fat to allow for healthy menstrual cycle function.

Being underweight or having a low percentage of body fat can cause long cycles, little cervical mucus, delayed ovulation, heavy or long periods, anovulatory cycles [27], short luteal phases, and amenorrhea [28]. To have normal menstrual cycles, Harvard researcher Rose E. Frisch, Ph.D. concluded that your body fat must contribute at least 22 percent to your total body weight [17]. Potential causes of low body fat include stress, vegetarian diets, smoking cigarettes, intestinal disorders, and heavy exercise. If low body fat causes amenorrhea, it increases the risk of bone mass loss and osteoporosis [27]. Being underweight and smoking may also increase suffering from menstrual cramps. Including fat in your diet to maintain an appropriate percentage of body fat is actually healthy and can improve menstrual cycle function and predictability. For some girls, gaining just 3-5 pounds can improve cycles and lead to shorter and lighter periods [27].

Talk to your doctor about a healthy weight and percentage body fat for you and to develop a plan to achieve and maintain your goal.

Illness

Illnesses can impact your cycle in similar ways as stress. Whether you get a common head cold, a stomach bug, a fever-inducing virus like the flu, or a bacterial infection like strep throat, your body's immune system must work overtime to try to return your body to good health. During this time, you may experience delayed ovulation or worsened premenstrual symptoms.

Another impact of illness may be your ability to observe your cycle signs. During a common head cold, you may experience a change in the quality or quantity of your mucus. A stomach virus accompanied by frequent diarrhea may make it difficult to make consistent observations of cervical mucus. And any viral or bacterial infection accompanied by a fever will throw off your basal body temperature observations. If your body does decide to ovulate in the middle of an illness, it may make it more difficult to observe a thermal shift and determine exactly when your luteal phase begins.

Jade's chart shows a potential impact of the common cold virus.

———————————————————— ✿ ————————————————————

Example # 21:   Cycle impacts of the Common Cold Illness

CYCLES & Spirituality

Name: Jade   My Typical Luteal Phase Length: 12-13 days   Age: 16   Year: 20XX   Chart #: 11

Jade had an extended time of wet/stretchy mucus on cycle days 11-21. During that time, she got a common cold virus accompanied by a runny nose, sore throat, sneezing, and coughing. The wet/stretchy cervical mucus she observed for many days in a row could have been influenced by the increased mucus drainage throughout her body caused by the cold. Since she observed a thermal shift in the middle of the wet/stretchy mucus, it is likely that Peak Day actually occurred somewhere in that timeframe and not actually on cycle day 21 as it seems on her chart. Jade noted breast tenderness on cycle days 16-17, which is right around the time of the thermal shift. It is likely that her true Peak Day and ovulation were closer to those days. Since her temperature observations seem to be unaffected by her cold, Jade could still accurately predict when her period would begin based on her known typical luteal phase length.

———————————————————— ✿ ————————————————————

Katie's chart shows an example of how a fever can impact cycle observations.

───────────────────────── ✿ ─────────────────────────

Example # 22: Cycle impacts of an Illness with Fever

	CYCLES & *Spirituality*																																					

Name: **Katie** — My Typical Luteal Phase Length **12 days** — Age **15** — Year **20XX** — Chart # **9**

Date	Day of month	10	11	12	13	14	15	16	17	18	19	20	21	22	23	24	25	26	27	28	29	30	31	1	2	3	4	5	6	7	8	9	10	11	12	13	14	15	16	17	18
	Month						January																					February													
	Day of week	S	M	T	W	R	F	S	S	M	T	W	R	F	S	S	M	T	W	R	F	S	S	M	T	W	R	F	S	S	M	T	W	R	F	S	S	M	T	W	R

Temperature (°F) — Normal Time I Measure Temperature: 5:45am

(temperature grid with plotted waking basal body temperatures; an "✖" mark placed over cycle days 15–16 indicating abnormal fever temperatures; Thermal Shift Line drawn at 97.3°F)

Cycle Day	1	2	3	4	5	6	7	8	9	10	11	12	13	14	15	16	17	18	(19)	20	21	22	23	24	25	26	27	28	29	30	31	32	33	34	35	36	37	38	39	40
Bleeding ● ○ ○	○	○	●	○	○	○																									○									
Mucus — wet / stretchy												▆	▆	▆	▆	▆	▆	▆																						
Mucus — damp / gooey			▆	▆	▆		▆	▆	▆	▆	▆								▆	▆	▆		▆																	
Mucus — dry / none																																								
Symptoms — physical symptoms, moods, impacts															strep throat				antibiotics (Jan 25 – Feb. 3)																					

On cycle days 15-16, Katie had strep throat accompanied by a fever. The fever impacted her waking basal body temperature on these days and she placed an " ✖ " over them to indicate she knew they were abnormal. On cycle day 16, she started treatment with antibiotics and on cycle day 17, her temperature was back to normal. This illness did not impact Katie's mucus observations and she observed Peak Day on cycle day 19. When Katie drew her Thermal Shift Line, she ignored the abnormally high temperatures on the days of fever and drew the line at 97.3°F, the highest temperature of the 6 days prior to the shift, not considering the abnormal days.

───────────────────────── ✿ ─────────────────────────

Underlying Health Concerns
Some recurrent patterns when charting your cycles may be signs of an underlying health concern. Identifying these concerns through your chart may help you obtain treatment for them earlier.

Vaginal Infections
Learning to identify your normal cervical mucus and how it changes throughout your cycle may help you more quickly identify abnormal vaginal discharges. Abnormal discharge may be itchy, resemble cottage cheese, have a foul odor, or be accompanied by irritation. If you experience abnormal vaginal discharge different from your typical cervical mucus, consult your doctor to rule out a vaginal infection, such as a yeast infection [29].

Thyroid Disorders
If your chart shows overall low basal body temperatures (hovering around 97.2°F or lower in the pre-ovulatory time), long cycles, heavy bleeding, or prolonged damp/gooey mucus, it may be a sign of hypothyroidism (an underactive thyroid) [24]. If you have other symptoms of hypothyroidism such as fatigue, weight gain, cold intolerance, constipation, dry skin, or thinning hair [30], you may want to investigate nutrition options to improve thyroid function which can lead to shorter and lighter periods [27] or discuss testing and treatment of hypothyroidism with your doctor.

Lyla's story

As I learned to chart my cycles, I quickly discovered in the first two cycles that my basal body temperatures were much lower than normal and my thermal shift wasn't very strong. Since I have a family history of thyroid issues, I talked to my doctor about thyroid testing. When my blood work revealed I was mildly hypothyroid, I learned that other symptoms of hypothyroidism probably explained why I was carrying extra body weight, despite being a frequent runner. Without charting my cycles, my symptoms weren't strong enough to motivate me to talk to my doctor. But once my hypothyroidism was treated, I saw noticeable improvements to my cycles, weight, and overall energy level.

Polycystic Ovary Syndrome

If your chart shows frequent long cycles, mucus that appears and disappears throughout the cycle, recurrent breakthrough bleeding [24], anovulatory cycles, prolonged periods, or a cycle greater than 90 days [19], especially if in combination with other symptoms such as acne, obesity, or excess hair growth in areas women do not usually have hair, it could be signs of Polycystic Ovary Syndrome (PCOS). PCOS is an endocrine system disorder usually associated with enlarged ovaries that contain small collections of fluid [31]. PCOS is found in 4% to 6% of adolescent girls [17]. If you have symptoms of PCOS, discuss diagnosis with your doctor since untreated PCOS can be a cause of future infertility. Consider the self-help strategies suggested in *Fertility, Cycles & Nutrition* by Marilyn Shannon. If you are considering surgical treatment for PCOS, a good source of information may be http://naprotechnology.com/.

Endometriosis

If your chart shows consistent heavy bleeding and painful periods with heavy cramping, first consider the natural treatments for menstrual symptoms discussed in the next chapter. If natural treatments do not reduce the severity of bleeding or cramping, it could be a sign of endometriosis. Endometriosis occurs when endometrial glands grow outside of the lining of the uterus, such as on the ovaries, behind the uterus, on the bowels, on the bladder, or rarely in other parts of the body. Approximately 4 to 17% of females who have reached menarche have endometriosis. Discuss possible symptoms of endometriosis with your doctor as untreated endometriosis can cause severe pain and infertility [17]. Consider the self-help strategies suggested in *Fertility, Cycles & Nutrition* by Marilyn Shannon. If you are considering surgical treatment for endometriosis, a good source of information may be http://naprotechnology.com/.

Medication Side Effects

Some medications, both over-the-counter and prescription, can impact your observable cycle signs [16]. Whether taken occasionally or long term, it is important to read the prescribing information and drug facts to be aware of side effects. Although most medication information sheets don't specifically state how the medicine may impact your observable cycle signs, you may be able to infer potential impacts to your cycle signs based on other stated side effects. For example, medications intended to dry up nasal drainage or oily skin or have a side effect of dry mouth may also dry up cervical mucus. Here are some common classes of medication and how they may impact your cycle signs.

Acne medications

Acne medications help dry up sebaceous glands in your skin and may have a similar drying effect on cervical mucus with results similar to antihistamines.

Antihistamines

Antihistamines, such as diphenhydramine, are frequently found in medicines used to treat colds, allergies, or insomnia. Since antihistamines help dry and thicken respiratory secretions [32], you may observe a similar drying effect on cervical mucus. Your cervical mucus may thicken or decrease in quantity. This drying effect on mucus may make it more difficult to observe wet/stretchy mucus and therefore to pinpoint a Peak Day in your cycle.

Antidepressants
Antidepressant medications may impact your cycle in a variety of ways. Read the prescribing information in detail for your particular medication to learn all possible side effects. Some cycle impacts from antidepressants may include delayed ovulation, amenorrhea (absence or cessation of ovulation & menstruation), breakthrough bleeding, and menorrhagia (excessive bleeding) [33].

Anti-diarrhea
Anti-diarrhea medications list dry mouth as one of the potential side effects [34]. This drying effect may also be observed on cervical mucus, similar to antihistamines.

Analgesics
Analgesic medications are used to treat mild to moderate pain and include aspirin and acetaminophen. These medications do not affect your observable cycle signs.

Anti-inflammatory agents, non-steroidal
Non-steroidal anti-inflammatory drugs (NSAIDs) are used to treat mild to moderate pain and inflammation and include common medications like ibuprofen and naproxen. NSAIDS affect blood clotting time and therefore may affect menstrual bleeding patterns [35]. They may potentially dry up cervical mucus.

Anti-Inflammatory Agents, Corticosteroids
Steroids include medications such as prednisone and methylprednisolone. In your body, steroids may resemble hormones and may affect your cycle signs by delaying ovulation or causing bleeding irregularities [36]. Short term treatments are less likely to impact your cycle but longer term treatment with steroids may impact your cycle signs for the duration of treatment.

Anti-Nausea
Anti-nausea medications list dry mouth as one of the potential side effects [37]. This drying effect may also be observed on cervical mucus, similar to antihistamines.

Expectorants
Expectorants, including guaifenesin, work by thinning bronchial mucus [38]. This thinning effect can also affect cervical mucus making it watery or stretchy. It will not produce more mucus but may thin the mucus already present.

Migraine Medications

Migraine medications typically list dry mouth as one of the potential side effects. This drying effect may also be observed on cervical mucus, similar to antihistamines.

Pain Control Agents

Pain medications, such as codeine, hydrocodone, and oxycodone, list dry mouth as one of the potential side effects. This drying effect may also be observed on cervical mucus, similar to antihistamines. Drinking lots of liquids may overcome the drying effect.

Thyroid Hormone

Thyroid hormone medications, including levothyroxine, that are used to treat hypothyroidism typically improve observable cycle signs. A woman with hypothyroidism who begins taking this class of medication may observe an increase in her overall basal body temperatures, a more regular pattern for cervical mucus, and shorter or more consistent cycle lengths [27].

This list of medications is not comprehensive. It does not include all medication classes and does not list all potential side effects or cycle impacts. When taking medications for any reason, be aware of how they impact your body and your cycle. If a medication is known or suspected to impact your cycle signs, it doesn't mean you should not take it. Consult with a doctor before starting or stopping taking any medications. If you and your doctor have determined that the benefits outweigh the risks of taking the medication, simply pay more attention to how your body may react. Note on your cycle chart when you begin taking any specific medication and when treatment ends. Make notes of any side effects or signs you observe. And always read the package insert or prescribing information.

Chapter 7 Summary

- Some factors can impact the timing of ovulation or the normal signs your body displays throughout your cycle. Charting can help you become more aware of things that may impact your cycle.

- Stress can impact your cycle by:
  - Delaying ovulation
  - Increasing premenstrual symptoms or affecting your ability to handle them

- A healthy body weight and percentage body fat can improve cycle regularity and reduce cycle symptoms.
  - Being overweight or having a high percentage of body fat may cause short luteal phases, amenorrhea, worsened PMS symptoms, and increased risk for uterine fibroids and breast cancer.
  - Being underweight or having a low percentage of body fat may cause long cycles, heavy or long periods, anovulatory cycles with breakthrough bleeding, and short luteal phases.

- Illnesses may impact your cycle or your cycle signs by:
  - Delaying ovulation
  - Changing your mucus pattern
  - Causing high temperature measurements during a fever

- Your chart may help you identify potential health concerns so you can discuss them with your doctor.

- Medications can impact your cycles or your cycle signs.
  - Always read the package insert or prescribing information to be aware of the potential side effects of medications you take.

"It is sown a natural body; it is raised a spiritual body. If there is a natural body, there is also a spiritual one."

1 Corinthians 15:44

Chapter 8:
Cycle Symptoms: Physical, Emotional, and Spiritual

Girls may experience a variety of symptoms associated with the various phases of their cycle. Some girls may only have few or occasional symptoms while some girls seem to be affected by every symptom every cycle. An estimated 20% to 40% of women have symptoms sufficiently bothersome enough to affect their relationships and job performance [17]. In this chapter, we'll discuss the physical and emotional symptoms related to your cycle and then provide suggestions for natural treatments and care.

Physical Symptoms
The typical physical symptoms of your menstrual cycle can include cramping, bloating, fatigue, breast tenderness, food cravings, skin problems, headache, and, of course, bleeding. This section describes and acknowledges each of these very real physical symptoms before we discuss how to naturally treat them in the next section.

Cramps and lower back pain
One of the most common symptoms of the menstrual cycle, especially for girls and younger women who have never given birth, is cramps. Teenage girls typically first begin to experience crampy lower abdominal pain with the onset of ovulatory cycles, usually 1-2 years following menarche. Research suggests cramps are physically caused by prostaglandins in menstrual fluid that induce smooth muscle contractions. Prostaglandin levels in menstrual fluid are higher in ovulatory cycles than in anovulatory cycles, explaining why some teenage girls may not experience cramps for their first several cycles following menarche [17]. Cramps can occur within a few days before your menstrual period and for the first few days during your menstrual period. Some girls feel cramps in their abdomen, lower back, or both. Premenstrual and menstrual cramps are a common symptom and many natural treatments (discussed in the next section) may provide relief. If menstrual cramps are severe or disabling and do not respond to natural treatment, you may need to see your doctor to determine if there is an underlying physical cause.

Some girls can also feel another type of cramping associated with ovulation pain, known as mittelschmerz. This sensation occurs around mid-cycle and can be an indication that ovulation is occurring. Ovulation pain can be mild or severe but is usually brief, lasting only a few minutes to 6-8 hours [17]. It may be felt on one side of the abdomen, depending on which ovary releases the egg that cycle.

Bloating, Water Retention, and Gastrointestinal Symptoms

Some girls may feel or even look bloated during certain times in their cycle. Bloating is retention of fluid and/or gas in the abdominal area. Bloating in the few days prior to your period or the first few days of your period is common. Some girls may experience bloating during the entire luteal phase (from after ovulation until their period begins). Being bloated can cause general discomfort by making your abdomen distended, your clothing feel tight, and your body pass gas. Diarrhea or constipation can also be premenstrual and menstrual symptoms.

Fatigue

Fatigue, tiredness, or lack of energy can be premenstrual or menstrual symptoms. It is not uncommon to feel like you need extra sleep or a nap on the days just prior to your period or the first few days of your period. Some girls may feel like they just don't have the energy to get up and do much of anything.

Breast Tenderness

Soreness, fullness, or pain in the breast tissue are some ways girls describe breast tenderness. Around the time of ovulation when estrogen production peaks, breast ducts enlarge. During the luteal phase when progesterone peaks, breast lobules (milk glands) grow [39]. If you are performing regular breast self-examinations, you may find that your breast tissue may feel more dense, rough, or bumpy in the outer areas around the time of ovulation or in the luteal phase which is why many health care professionals recommend performing breast self-exams near the beginning of your cycle, just after your period. Some girls also experience sensitive nipples as a premenstrual, menstrual, or ovulation symptom.

Food Cravings

Some girls experience food cravings during the few days prior to and first few days of menstruation. The types of foods each girl craves may be different. Some typical food cravings associated with premenstrual syndrome include "comfort foods", chocolate, or sugar.

Skin Problems

Teenagers in particular are more likely to experience skin changes associated with their cycle. The most common problem, acne, can flare up around the time of ovulation, just prior to or the first few days of your period, or even for the entire luteal phase.

Headache

Changes in the level of estrogen hormone during the menstrual cycle are associated with headaches. Just prior to menstruation, estrogen levels drop to their lowest levels of your cycle. Some girls experience headaches as a premenstrual symptom. Girls who are susceptible to migraines may see them onset or worsen during the premenstrual time [40]. Some girls may experience nervousness or dizziness as premenstrual or menstrual symptoms [17].

Spotting

Spotting is considered to be very light bleeding from your vagina and may be light pink, red, or brown in color. Some girls may have spotting at the beginning or end of their period. Some girls experience spotting around the time of ovulation.

Bleeding

Bleeding from the vagina approximately two weeks after ovulation is known as menstruation. Bleeding can be light, moderate, or heavy on different days of your cycle. Many girls find this symptom the most difficult to deal with because feminine products must be changed often enough to stay hygienic and activities such as swimming require additional products or precautions.

Bleeding at other times during your cycle not preceded by ovulation is typically known as breakthrough bleeding. Breakthrough bleeding is common for the first few years following menarche. If breakthrough bleeding occurs frequently or for several cycles in a row once ovulatory cycles have been established, you may need to discuss potential causes with your doctor.

Very heavy bleeding is considered to be soaking a regular absorbency maxi pad (not a thin pad) or tampon in less than 2 hours [19] or passing blot clots greater than 1 inch in diameter [41]. Blood flow of greater than 8-10 days is considered excessive [17]. If you experience very heavy bleeding, excessive bleeding, or bleeding that is debilitating or associated with excessive pain, consult your doctor.

Emotional Symptoms

Have you ever snapped at your parents or friends for something petty and realized only in retrospect (once your period actually started) that maybe you had been jumpy due to PMS? The emotional symptoms of PreMenstrual Syndrome (PMS) can include depression, angry outbursts, irritability, crying spells, anxiety, confusion, social withdrawal, poor concentration, insomnia, and increased nap taking [42].

As we discussed in Chapter 3, the four key female hormones (estrogen, progesterone, FSH, and LH) are constantly changing throughout the cycle. These changing levels of hormones can impact your emotional state. While changing hormone levels do affect mood and contribute to emotional symptoms, if you are empowered with the knowledge of your body you are more likely to understand and acknowledge your emotions without letting them get the best of you.

Simply being aware of where you are in your cycle can help you identify when your emotions, attitude, and mood may be related to your fluctuating hormones. For most girls, the biggest emotional roller coaster begins a few days before their period when estrogen and progesterone levels rapidly drop. If you know from your chart when you have ovulated and when to expect your period, you can mentally prepare to keep the snappiness in-check.

Have you ever noticed yourself becoming emotional as if you have PMS but thinking it can't be related since your period is still a week or two away? For many girls, the up-and-down emotions of "PreMenstrual Syndrome" can also occur around ovulation or throughout the entire luteal phase when all four key hormones are changing dramatically.

Natural Treatments & Care

Through charting your cycles, you will begin to learn when certain physical and emotional symptoms typically impact your own cycle and can take action to help alleviate or prevent them altogether. Cycles are a natural part of God's design for girls and learning to deal with them can have an impact on the rest of your life.

Lindsey's story

Throughout my teenage and young-adult years, I dreaded my period. Really dreaded it. Over the years, I tried many forms of hormones to try to reduce the impact of my cycles on my life, including several versions of the Pill and Intra-Uterine Devices (IUDs). After I was married and had children, I realized the many side effects of the hormones I had taken and finally decided to go back to natural cycles. Learning to deal with natural cycles when I was in my mid-thirties was not easy and I still don't look forward to my period. Finding ways to manage the symptoms has helped and I hope that other girls learn to deal in healthier ways physically and emotionally at a younger age.

Here are several natural remedies for premenstrual symptoms. Discover the ones that work for you.

Exercise

You have probably heard that exercise is good for cramps. But will running a marathon or playing basketball make you cramp-free? Probably not. Getting regular exercise most days of the week such as brisk walking, bicycling, swimming, or general aerobic activity can help alleviate symptoms such as fatigue and mood [43]. But all exercise is not equal for reducing cramps or bloating. By understanding your body's mechanics, you can choose the right kind of exercise to target the muscles around the uterus. Certain yoga poses, Clinical Somatic movements, Pilates movements, and ballet positions that are designed based on body mechanics may help relax the uterus and reduce cramping in the abdomen and lower back. Similar body positions and movements can also help activate the digestive system to reduce the fluid and air retention that cause bloating.

One of the more simple yoga poses, known as Cat & Cow, may help reduce cramping, lower back pain, bloating, or abdominal discomfort associated with your menstrual cycle. Although traditional yoga has some religious aspects that are not in unison with Christian beliefs, performing the poses alone (without incantations or meditations) is simply exercise for your body. To perform Cat & Cow, use these steps:

1. Begin on all fours with your wrists in line with your shoulders and your knees in line with your hips. Begin with your back flat and your neck in a long and neutral position.
2. As you inhale, let your belly drop and fill with air, *slowly* arch your back, and lift your head slightly so the gaze of your eyes is toward the ceiling.
3. As you exhale, *slowly* round your spine, drop your head so the gaze of your eyes is toward your navel, and expel all the air out of your belly while you tighten your abdominal muscles.
4. Perform the movement slowly and with long, full breaths. Repeat the movement with each inhale and exhale for 5-10 breaths. After the final exhale, return to the starting neutral position.

You can also modify this exercise to use while sitting in a chair.

A restful yoga pose, known as Child's Pose, may also help reduce cramping and lower back aches. To perform Child's Pose, use these steps:

1. Begin on all fours with your knees hip-width apart and the tops of your feet touching the floor. (After you've tried hip-width, you can try a slightly wider stance of the knees to determine which pose brings greater relief to your own body.)
2. As you exhale, slowly lower your bottom towards your heels.

116

3. Lengthen your neck and rest your forehead on the floor.
4. Lay your arms by your side with palms facing up. Or, for Extended Child's Pose, lengthen your arms above your head with your palms touching the floor.
5. Breathe with long, full breaths that expand your abdomen and lower back as you rest.

You can also modify this exercise by tucking your toes under and sticking your bottom up in the air to feel a greater release in your lower back [44].

Other yoga poses that may help relieve menstrual discomfort are Bridge Pose, Half-Moon Pose, and Reclining Angle Bound Pose [17].

A movement used in Clinical Somatics, called Arch & Flatten [44, 45], also targets the abdominal muscles to help reduce cramping, lower back pain, bloating, or abdominal discomfort associated with your menstrual cycle. To perform Arch & Flatten, use these steps:
1. Lay on your back with your knees bent and your feet flat on the floor. Lightly place your hands on your lower abdomen on the area you desire to target.
2. As you inhale slowly, fill your abdomen with air and allow it to inflate like a balloon. Allow your pelvis to roll downward slightly toward your tail bone, gently arch your lower back, and rock your head slightly back to raise your chin toward the ceiling.
3. As you exhale slowly, sink your abdomen down, allowing it to flatten as it expels out air. Roll your pelvis upward and imagine your abdomen is scooped out in the area between your belly button and pelvis. If you can, tighten the muscles of your pelvic floor. Rock your head back down to slightly tuck your chin.
4. Repeat this Arch & Flatten movement slowly and gently. As your back and abdominal area begin to warm up, gradually increase the range of the "inchworm" motion. Repeat the movement with each inhale and exhale for 8-10 breaths. After the final exhale, lengthen your legs out straight and your arms above your head for a gentle full body lengthening stretch.

Exercises to target the deep abdominal muscles can also be performed with an exercise ball. Vivian Stooke, certified Pilates instructor, Clinical Somatics instructor, and owner of Form Studio [44], instructs her clients to perform the exercises using very slow movements.

1. Lay on your back with your knees bent and your ankles resting on the top of the exercise ball (choose a ball size that allows your knees to form a 90-degree angle when in this position).
2. Inhale to prepare. As you exhale, use your lower, deep abdominal muscles to slowly roll the ball and bring your legs toward your chest. If you can, tighten the muscles of your pelvic floor.
3. Inhale as you slowly return your legs and the ball to the original extended position.
4. Repeat this legs-to-chest movement slowly with each breath for about 8 breaths.

Girls who practice ballet may find that their barre routine or other movements that target their core muscles help reduce cramping [44].

Makayla's story
I am a ballet dancer.
Anytime I am feeling crampy, it helps SO much to go to the studio and do basic ballet movements that activate my core muscles.

An ancient Chinese exercise called Ba Duan Jin has also been studied to improve premenstrual syndrome symptoms [46]. Ba Duan Jin is a sequence of eight movements that takes about five to ten minutes to perform.

Consult with your doctor before starting or stopping any exercise routine.

Healthy foods

What you eat can have a large impact on your physical health and how you feel at all times during your cycle, but especially during the premenstrual and menstrual times. Eating healthy can reduce cramps, bloating, fatigue, and even heavy bleeding! A healthy diet consists of vegetables & fruits, whole grains, dairy, meat & protein, and even fats but limits sugar and foods that cause spikes in your blood sugar levels.

A balanced healthy diet is not common in our American way of life. With our busy lifestyles, it is tempting to grab pre-packaged snacks and meals prepared at restaurants. As a young woman, now is a great time to adopt healthy eating habits! If you still live at home with your family, get involved in meal planning and make small changes at a time. Volunteer to make a salad to go along with dinner for your family. Or wake up a few minutes early to make scrambled eggs to add to your usual high-carbohydrate breakfast. If you live on your own, stock your pantry with healthy foods that make it easier to make healthy choices. Consider having your friends over on a Friday night to socialize and cook a meal together instead of going out to eat. To improve your diet, talk with your doctor and/or a dietician and consider making some of the following changes:

- Eat more vegetables and fruits. Some PMS symptoms have been linked to low levels of vitamins and minerals [47] and colorful fruits and vegetables are full of vitamins, minerals, fiber, and phytonutrients your body needs to function. They are truly natural wonders grown from God's earth. Eat a variety and be willing to try new foods. Taste buds change as you get older so you may actually enjoy vegetables you hated as a kid! To add as many vegetables as you can, try a salad at lunch time (with protein like meats, beans, or nuts and salad dressing containing healthy fats), snack on raw veggies (along with protein), and fill half your dinner plate with gently-cooked vegetables. Since many fruits contain a fair amount of sugar, eat fruits along with other food groups (like protein, fat, and whole grains) that can help prevent spikes in your blood sugar. Add berries to your creamy oatmeal for breakfast and make a snack of apples or bananas along with nuts or cheese. Frozen vegetables and fruits are a healthy alternative when fresh options are not available. A high intake of vegetables and fruits may help reduce menstrual cramps [48].

- Eat your grains whole. Whole grains are grains grown, harvested, and then eaten without refining. Whole grains include whole wheat, brown rice, quinoa, millet, barley, and oats. They can be used to make delicious foods such as whole-grain bread, whole-wheat pasta, oatmeal, and side-dishes for dinner and they can be added to soups and salads. Whole grains are plant foods and provide vitamins, minerals, and nutrients. Whole grains help stabilize blood sugar levels. Grains that have been processed (such as white flour) and stripped of nutrients and fiber are of little nutritional value. In your body, white flour acts similarly to sugar causing large spikes followed by rapid drops in blood sugar levels. Though whole grains are considered "carbohydrates", our bodies process whole grains slower and without disrupting blood sugar levels as severely as when we eat white bread, white pasta, and white rice. To implement this change in your diet, read ingredient labels and choose foods with a whole grain as the first ingredient (for example, choose breads made with whole wheat flour instead of enriched wheat flour).

- Include protein. Although many Americans get more than enough protein in their diets, certain groups of people may need to focus more on including protein, particularly girls who are vegetarian, restrict calories, or crave and consume a mostly carbohydrate diet during PMS. Protein is essential for proper function of muscle tissue, skin cells, and bones. Protein, in combination with whole grains, helps slow the release of glucose (sugar) into the blood which can contribute to steady blood sugar levels instead of spikes and dips that can cause hypoglycemia. Eat some protein with every meal and snack. Foods that are good sources of protein include animal products (dairy, eggs, fish, poultry, and red meat) as well as beans, nuts, and lentils.

- Don't eliminate fat. Your body actually needs fat to function properly. Fat helps provide energy, helps your body absorb vitamins, makes you feel full longer, and is essential for brain function. The benefits and downsides of the different types of fats and the proper ratio to consume them are a current area of interest for medical researchers. Here are some points of interest in the published literature.

  o Monounsaturated fats. Monounsaturated fats are also known as the "good fats". Monounsaturated fats improve blood cholesterol levels, blood sugar control [49], vitamin absorption, immune system function, and cell health [27]. Monounsaturated fats are found in many foods but have particularly high concentrations in olive oil, macadamia nuts, almonds, cashews, peanuts, and

120

avocados. To increase monounsaturated fats in your diet, snack on nuts, indulge in guacamole, and soak up the olive oil on your whole grain bread. Monounsaturated fats like olive oil are also one of the best choices for cooking because they do not degrade with high heat [50, 51].

o Polyunsaturated, omega-3, and omega-6 fatty acids. Polyunsaturated fats is a broad term that includes some fats agreed to be excellent for your health and others with recent research showing potential negative impacts on your health in large doses. Similar to monounsaturated fats, polyunsaturated fats aid in vitamin absorption, immune system function, and healthy cells [27]. Omega-3 and omega-6 fatty acids are two types of polyunsaturated fats and are known as "essential fatty acids" because they are essential to your diet since your body does not make them by itself. The essential fatty acids are particularly beneficial to your cycle health [27].

   ▪ Omega-3 fatty acids can help boost brain function [52], help control acne [53], contribute to healthy cycles [27], improve your mood [52] and improve breast cancer prognosis [54]. Omega-3 fatty acids may reduce menstrual pain [55, 56] and help girls with PCOS have more regular cycles [57]. Omega-3 fats are ones you don't want to cut back on. Good food sources of omega-3 fatty acids are wild Alaskan salmon, walnuts, and flaxseed oil.
   ▪ Omega-6 fatty acids aid in brain function, promote normal development, and reduce inflammation [58]. Food sources of omega-6 fatty acids are sunflower oil, safflower oil, corn oil, soy oil, and canola oil. Although omega-6 fatty acids are essential to our diet, most Americans get far more than enough because the foods we tend to eat have a high concentration of these oils. An overabundance of certain omega-6 fats can increase inflammation [58] and increase the risk of breast cancer [59]. Additionally, heating polyunsaturated fats as cooking oils can cause them to degrade into toxic compounds [50].
   ▪ Our bodies need a balance of omega-3 and omega-6 fatty acids in about equal amounts which, for most Americans, means not actively adding any additional omega-6 sources to our diet but striving to increase omega-3 sources [58].

o Saturated fats. Though saturated fats have been labeled "bad fats", their 'bad rap' is being overturned with new research [60]. When we try to reduce the amount of saturated fat in our diet and instead replace it with carbohydrates, we actually increase our risk of cardiovascular disease, obesity, and diabetes [61]. Replacing saturated fats with polyunsaturated fats may have a similar association [62]. Saturated fat actually has important health benefits, including absorption of certain fat-soluble vitamins [27]. If you currently eat a low-fat diet, consider including some natural sources of saturated fat in your diet like whole milk, full-fat yogurt, cheese, real butter, and coconut oil. A large study associated consumption of at least two servings of high fat dairy products with lower rates of anovulatory cycles [63]. (Dairy products are also a good source of dietary calcium, which can reduce PMS [64].) Coconut oil is also a good source of saturated fat, in particular medium chain triglycerides, that can help our bodies fight illnesses, positively affect thyroid function, control blood sugar, improve cholesterol, and control body fat [65]. Coconut oil is also excellent for cooking as it does not degrade with high heat [66].

o Trans fats. Artificial trans fats are formed when liquid oils are partially hydrogenated and turned into solid fats, such as shortening or margarine. Artificial trans fats are man-made and are intended to make processed foods more "shelf-stable" to extend their edible "life". But that also makes them have a longer "life" inside our bodies and accumulate throughout our lives. In making trans fats, the essential fatty acids are destroyed. Trans fats are found in margarine and shortening and any foods cooked in or baked with these fats. The US Food and Drug Administration (FDA) has acknowledged that trans fats raise LDL ("bad cholesterol"), lower HDL ("good cholesterol") and increase the risk of heart disease. The FDA no longer considers trans fats as "Generally Recognized as Safe" [67] and requires food labels to list the amount of trans fats per serving in the food. However, Nutrition Fact labels can state "0 grams trans fats per serving" even when the food contains trans fats. To determine with certainty if a food contains any trans fats at all, scan the ingredients list for the words "partially hydrogenated". Avoid all trans fats.

- Limit sugar. Sweet, sugary foods (like candy, cake, cookies, and pastries) are typically high in calories and low in nutrients. Consuming foods and beverages high in sugar, especially on an empty stomach, causes surges in your body's blood sugar levels followed by drastic drops in blood sugar as your body processes the high sugar load. Studies show that women who experience PMS typically eat more sugar in their diets [27]. Repeated spikes and dips in your blood sugar can cause abnormally low blood glucose levels, a condition known as hypoglycemia. Hypoglycemia can bring feelings of shakiness, fatigue, irritability, anxiety, clumsiness, and even blurred vision. Low blood sugar levels are associated with painful periods [68]. A high intake of added sugar can also increase your risk of cardiovascular disease [69] and diabetes. Limiting sugary foods (and replacing them with meals and snacks that help maintain steady blood sugar levels) is best for your overall health and for reducing menstrual symptoms. Occasionally indulging in a treat can be satisfying but do so on a full stomach. Eating dessert immediately after a meal (such as following a dinner rich in protein, fat, whole grains, and vegetables) can be less harmful as it helps slow the absorption of sugar into the blood. When your stomach is full of healthy foods, it may also help your brain control the portion size of your sugary dessert.

- Reduce (or eliminate!) processed foods. Processed foods are those that have been greatly altered from the form God gave them to us. This can apply to foods from fried fast foods to boxed cereals and packaged pastries. Processed foods often contain trans fats, white or bleached flour, artificial ingredients, additives, preservatives, and too many calories without providing many vitamins or nutrients. There are plenty of tasty and healthy choices to replace a toaster pastry breakfast!

- Drink plenty of water. Staying hydrated by drinking water may reduce the pain of menstrual cramps. Avoid soft drinks which can increase blood sugar levels (even artificially sweetened ones) [70]. Drink enough water each day to quench your thirst and stay hydrated, especially the few days prior to your period.

- Avoid caffeine. Cut back on coffee (even decaffeinated coffee, which still contains some caffeine), caffeinated tea, and caffeinated soda, especially in the days before your period begins, as caffeine can contribute to mood and energy level disturbances [47] and can increase breast tenderness [39]. A study of young women associated premenstrual symptoms with daily consumption of caffeinated beverages. There was a definite effect at just one serving per day and symptoms increased in severity with greater consumption [71]. Note that some over-the-counter pain relief medications marketed for menstrual symptoms contain caffeine [72], which may be counter-productive for treating some PMS symptoms.

- Limit salt and salty foods. Though sodium is essential for your body to control blood pressure and blood volume and for your muscles and nerves to function properly [73], too much salt can contribute to bloating and fluid retention [47]. Foods containing too much salt can include canned soups, canned or jarred tomato sauces, processed foods, and foods prepared at a restaurant. If you experience bloating, reduce the consumption of these high-sodium foods (but don't eliminate sodium completely) shortly before your period begins [74].

- Eat smaller, more frequent meals. Try eating four to six smaller meals per day, or about every 3 hours, instead of filling up to capacity with three large meals per day [17]. Large portions can contribute to bloating and can also cause spikes in your body's sugar levels.

- Try to get your vitamins from your diet. Diets rich in the B vitamins thiamine and riboflavin (found in meats, beans, spinach, and whole grains) lower the risk of PMS [75]. A high intake of calcium and vitamin D from food sources (like dairy) may reduce the risk of PMS [64]. High dietary intakes of iron (found especially in red meats, beans, eggs, spinach, and raisins) may be associated with a lower risk of PMS [76] and lighter periods [77]. Foods rich in Vitamin C (including red peppers, citrus fruits, kiwi, broccoli, and tomato juice) can aid in the absorption of iron in the body [78]. Foods rich in Vitamin K (such as leafy green vegetables) or probiotics (found in yogurts with live active bacteria) can help lighten and shorten menstrual bleeding [27]. Striving to eat a healthy and varied diet will provide many of these vitamins naturally and may help improve symptoms related to your cycle.

124

Natural and Organic Foods to Limit Artificial Hormones

As the graphs in Chapter 3 show, the fluctuating hormones in your body are enough to impact your emotions by themselves. Don't add to them! When possible, avoid adding extra hormones to your body via your foods.

- <u>Choose organic, when possible</u>. There are many different reasons to consider eating organic foods. The main reason relating to your cycle is that organic foods do not contain genetically-modified ingredients, artificial ingredients (such as colors, flavors, sweeteners, or preservatives), added hormones, or pesticides which may disrupt normal hormonal activity. Organic foods are typically more expensive than non-organic foods so if you are on a limited budget, select organic for foods that make the biggest impact. These include foods you eat a lot of, dairy products, and fruits and vegetables known to absorb high levels of pesticides. (Find the most recent list of foods high in pesticides at the Environmental Working Group website: www.ewg.org/foodnews/) [79].

- <u>Choose hormone-free beef</u>. In the United States, it is common practice to increase the growth rate and meat production of animals, particularly beef cattle and sheep, with the use of steroid hormone drugs, including natural and synthetic estrogen, progesterone, and testosterone [80]. Although the FDA has approved these drugs and reports that the levels of hormones in meat are safe for people to eat because the same hormones are found naturally in humans, residues of added hormones in meat are up to 20-fold higher than normally-occurring levels of hormones [81]. Scientific literature reports evidence to correlate added hormones in meat with the rise in the incidence of hormone-related cancers such as breast and prostate cancers [82]. Europe and Japan have banned hormone-raised beef. Understanding how the natural hormones in our own female bodies function and vary, it is not difficult to postulate that adding external hormones to our bodies via foods could disrupt our cycles. When choosing meat from the grocery store, select beef that is hormone-free. Beef that is certified as "USDA Organic" is also hormone-free. At restaurants in the United States, assume all beef contains hormones unless it specifically states otherwise.

- <u>Choose hormone-free milk and dairy</u>. In the United States since 1993, the FDA has allowed dairy cows to be injected with the genetically-engineered artificial hormone rBGH (recombinant bovine growth hormone), also known as rBST (recombinant bovine somatotropin), to increase milk production. The FDA states that no significant difference has been found between milk derived from rBST-treated and non-rBST treated cows and that food products from cows treated with rBGH are safe for consumption by humans. This finding is based largely on a short and limited study on rats [83]. The FDA's approval does not address long-term human exposure to artificial hormones or their impacts on hormone-related cancers or women's hormonal cycles. Studies show that milk from cows treated with rBGH contains higher levels of IGF-1 (Insulin Growth Factor-1). Elevated levels of IGF-1 in humans have been linked to colon and breast cancer. Europe, Japan, Australia, New Zealand, and Canada do not allow the use of rBGH [84]. When choosing milk, yogurt, cheese, sour cream, ice cream, and other dairy products from the grocery store, select products that specifically state "rBGH-free" or "rBST-free". Dairy products that are certified as "USDA Organic" are also free of artificial hormones.

- <u>Limit whole soy foods</u>. Soy foods contain isoflavones, which are estrogen-like compounds. Research seems unclear as to whether or not these estrogenic foods affect the level of estrogen or other hormones in the body. However, it is known that soy foods can interfere with healthy thyroid function, which is a common cause of cycle irregularity [27]. Limit or avoid consumption of unfermented whole soy products such as soy milk, tofu, soy drinks, or soy protein products. On the other hand, soy oil and fermented soy products such as tempeh, miso, and soy sauce do not contain the hormone-disrupting agents of whole soy products [85].

Vitamins & Supplements

Despite eating as healthily as we can, our modern diet is often not varied enough or adequate to fully provide all of the vitamins, minerals, and nutrients our bodies need. Wholesome foods are best but our modern lifestyle practically dictates that we can't eat perfect. To make up for the nutrients we don't get enough of, supplementing with vitamins, minerals, and essential fatty acids can help improve your overall health and your cycles, including periods that are lighter and less painful. You may want to consider a daily multi-vitamin and/or specific vitamin supplements known to help cycle-related issues such as cramps, bloating, fatigue, and heavy periods [86]. Consult your doctor or health care professional before taking vitamins or supplements.

- Calcium. Calcium may reduce the physical and psychological symptoms of PMS [17, 87]. Women ages 9-18 need approximately 1300 mg of calcium per day and women ages 19-50 need approximately 1000 mg of calcium per day [88]. A high intake of calcium may not only reduce premenstrual symptoms but may also reduce the risk of developing premenstrual symptoms in the future in girls who do not currently have symptoms [64]. If you are not getting enough calcium in your diet, consider a daily calcium supplement that also contains vitamin D for better absorption.

- Magnesium. In order to absorb the calcium in your food and/or supplements more effectively, your body also needs magnesium. Taking magnesium supplements before your period begins and during it may help reduce water retention, breast tenderness, bloating, and mood symptoms [17, 42, 47]. Magnesium may also reduce painful periods [89]. For cramping, taking 200 mg of magnesium every two hours (up to 1,000 mg per day) may be helpful [86]. Chocolate contains magnesium and some researchers believe that chocolate cravings prior to menstruation may be a sign of a magnesium deficiency [90].

- Vitamin E. The American College of Obstetricians and Gynecologists and the Mayo Clinic recommend Vitamin E to ease the PMS symptoms of cramping and breast tenderness [42, 47]. A study of teenage girls concluded that Vitamin E relieves the pain of periods and reduces blood loss [91].

- Vitamin A. Supplements of Vitamin A may help reduce heavy bleeding [27, 92]. Beta-carotene is the most natural form of Vitamin A. If the supplement contains Vitamin A as Retinyl Palmitate, check with your doctor to determine the recommended maximum dosage.

- Vitamin B6. Supplements of Vitamin B6 can help lengthen and stabilize the luteal phase of your cycle and can reduce the symptoms of PMS, especially anxiety [27]. Clinical trials suggest up to 100 mg of Vitamin B6 daily are likely to have a beneficial effect on premenstrual symptoms and premenstrual depression [93].

- Vitamin C and bioflavonoids. Supplements of Vitamin C in combination with bioflavonoids can help reduce menstrual bleeding [27]. Vitamin C also helps improve the absorption of iron, which may be low in women with heavy bleeding.

- Fish oil, flax oil, and fatty acids. Supplements of fish oil or flax oil containing omega-3 fatty acids can help reduce cramps and reduce heavy or prolonged bleeding [94]. Flaxseed supplementation has been associated with longer luteal phases [95]. A study in the journal *Reproductive Health* found that women who took a supplement of essential fatty acids (that included gamma linolenic acid, oleic acid, linoleic acid, other polyunsaturated acids, and vitamin E) significantly reduced PMS symptoms [96].

- Chlorophyll capsules. Chlorophyll provides Vitamin K. During heavy periods, 30-50mg chlorophyll capsules taken 1-3 times per day only during days of heavy bleeding can help lighten bleeding within an hour [86].

Maria's story

I try to eat a healthy and balanced diet including whole grains, vegetables, fruits, plenty of dairy (I LOVE yogurt and ice cream!), and meat. Even so, I decided to try some vitamin supplements and was surprised by how much better I felt! For me, magnesium really helped my PMS symptoms (I probably needed it to balance all the calcium I get from dairy) and I believe the multi-vitamin actually made my irregular cycles somewhat more "regular".

Home Remedies
Occasionally despite regular exercise, healthy eating, and vitamin supplements to improve your overall health throughout your cycle, you may still need immediate relief from painful cramps on the worst day. In those instances, try these home remedies:

- Warm heat. Place a warm heat pack (such as a heating pad or microwaveable moist heat pack) on your lower back or abdomen.

- Warm bath. Sitting in a warm bath may help reduce cramps (and help you relax). Adding magnesium salt (i.e. Epsom salt) to the bath water may also help relax muscles and may even increase magnesium levels in the body [97]. Consider avoiding bubble baths, however, as soaking in strong surfactants may irritate the vaginal area.

- Massage. Gently massaging your lower back or abdomen may provide physical relief. You can ask a close friend or family member for a gentle massage or give it a try yourself!

- Hot liquids. Drinking hot liquids such as tea, water, or even hot lemonade can increase blood flow and relax muscles that cramp. But do avoid caffeine as it can increase nervous energy and make menstrual cramps worse.

Herbal Treatments
Some women report PMS relief using herbal treatments though no large scientific studies have confirmed their effectiveness. Peppermint may help reduce bloating and gas, relax muscles, and relieve headaches [98]. Chasteberry may help breast tenderness, acne [99], mood, headache, bloating, breast pain [17] [20, 43], and heavy bleeding [77]. Raspberry leaf tea may help reduce menstrual cramps [100]. Black cohosh [101], dandelion, and evening primrose oil may also reduce PMS [102]. Ginger may help reduce heavy bleeding [77]. However, herbal remedies are not regulated by the Food and Drug Administration, so product safety and effectiveness are unknown, especially with long-term use [47]. Consult your doctor regarding the efficacy of herbal treatments and possible risks.

Stress Reduction

Stress affects our body in many ways: causing fatigue, raising heart rate and blood pressure, and making us feel anxious or irritated. Stress can also increase the symptoms of PMS and make these symptoms more difficult to deal with. Stress, life crisis events, and low self-esteem can increase the severity of cramping and painful menstruation [17].

Certainly stress can be caused by emotional events or life situations. But underlying sources of stress are often physical stresses such as illness, allergies, poor nutrition, lack of exercise, overexertion, or lack of sleep. Addressing these physical stresses may improve your energy and ability to handle PMS and the everyday emotional stresses life brings [27].

Getting enough sleep is important. Although you may be able to "function" on 6-7 hours of sleep each night, your body may need closer to 8-9 hours [103] of sleep per night to feel well-rested and reduce stress. Lack of sleep raises anxiety. Sleep lowers cortisol, the stress hormone [104]. A sleep routine – where you wake up and go to sleep at the same times every day, even on the weekends – may help lessen moodiness and fatigue [42].

If stress is severely impacting your life in a negative way, seek professional help.

Acknowledging Your Emotions

If you've ever had the experience of one of your closest family members or friends trying to "diagnose" your bad mood (surely they mean well) by accusing you of having PMS, your instinctive reaction may have been defensive. Not many people want to admit, especially to others, when their emotions are out of control.

The best way to handle the emotional symptoms associated with fluctuating hormones in your cycle is to first acknowledge they exist. Scientifically, medical research shows how female hormones fluctuate so you can rest assured it's not just you! But the real acknowledgement comes when we think about our own emotions individually.

Charting your cycle can give you a profound since of emotional awareness. Knowing where you are in your cycle and how drastically your hormones may be fluctuating can allow you to reflect on the reasons for your emotions.

If you find yourself crying alone in your bedroom for no apparent reason, allow some time for quiet introspection. Acknowledge that there is likely nothing "wrong" with you and that your crying or sadness may be due to hormonal fluctuations associated with your cycle. Allow yourself a few moments to "cry it out" and then try to focus your mind on more healthy thoughts. In quiet personal moments like these, some girls find it helpful to journal their dreams, write poetry, draw, practice playing a musical instrument, read a book, or think of something kind to do for others. If we can find ways to turn our emotions into quiet, positive reflection, it can provide us with much-needed "downtime" from our typically hectic lives.

If you find yourself snapping back at your family or friends with short, sarcastic, or even rude comments, try to take pause for a moment and bite your tongue before the conversation escalates. Acknowledge (to yourself) that your reaction may be related to your hormonal fluctuations. Consider excusing yourself from the situation and taking some quiet time to calm down. Later, out of the heat of the moment, a simple "I'm sorry" may smooth things over with the forgiving people closest to you.

If your emotions become uncontrollable, lead to depression, or cause you to have negative thoughts about your life, talk to someone you love and can trust to help you seek professional help immediately.

Spiritual Reflection

When dealing with both the physical and emotional symptoms of your menstrual cycle, your spirituality can be a powerful source for natural treatment [17]. Take time to be in quiet and reflect that your body is functioning in God's natural design. Just like the seasons of nature, our bodies cycle for a reason. After a long cold winter, spring is always a joyous time of budding new life. After a hot and humid summer, the brilliant colors and pleasant temperatures of fall can be heart-warming. The changes our bodies go through each cycle can help us appreciate the many aspects of our complex lives and God's design. Each cycle, our bodies prepare to bring children into the world. Until and if we are called to marriage and motherhood, we can anticipate with awe and wonder what that miracle will be like.

During tough times physically and emotionally, prayer can bring peace and strengthen your mental ability to accept reality and deal with problems. Prayer can even result in miraculous healing. Try out various forms of prayer to find the best way you connect with God. Consider prayers like the Our Father, meditation, prayer in the form of song, or a casual spontaneous conversation. Asking for God's help during difficult times can also bring us closer to God and remind us to thank him during the wonderful times!

During spiritual reflection regarding your cycle, it can help to remember that you are not alone in this journey of womanhood. Many women throughout centuries have experienced the same physical and emotional discomforts you are experiencing. Consider how women of biblical times dealt with menstruation without the modern conveniences of sanitary pads, toilets, or even running water! Contemplate the many female Saints and the remarkable lives they led, all while dealing with the same hormonal fluctuations we encounter. Wonder with amazement how Mary, the mother of Jesus, dealt with premenstrual symptoms while raising her Son. Looking at the lives of these women, you will find no shortage of inspiration.

Veronica's story

In the few days before my period and the first few days of my period, I sometimes find myself in a more solemn state. I tend to be quiet, contemplative, and reflective. In these times, I am also more observant of nature and find connection with God in that way. I appreciate God's beautiful creations when I notice brightly colored flowers. I feel God's power during thunderstorms. I find it a good time to recenter my life.

Noting Natural Treatments Helpful to Me

As you chart your cycles and begin to try some of the natural treatments and self-care to help reduce your cycle symptoms, make notes on your chart regarding what works for you. Each girl may find different treatments helpful for different symptoms. When you find what works for your unique body, write it down in the "Care" section at the bottom of the chart. Then when you experience similar symptoms during your next few cycles, you can look back to previous cycles for your own suggestions.

In the following example, Grace notes particular exercises, vitamins, and moments of spiritual reflection that seemed to help during this cycle and makes a note to herself to try to adjust her diet during her next cycle.

Example # 23: Making Note of Helpful Treatments

CYCLES & Spirituality

Name: **Grace** My Typical Luteal Phase Length: **12 days** Age: **18** Year: **20XX** Chart #: **7**

Date	Day of month	22	23	24	25	26	27	28	29	30	1	2	3	4	5	6	7	8	9	10	11	12	13	14	15	16	17	18	19	20	21	22	23	24	25	26	27	28		
	Month	September									October																													
	Day of week	T	W	R	F	S	S	M	T	W	R	F	S	S	M	T	W	R	F	S	S	M	T	W	R	F	S	S	M	T	W	R	F	S	S	M	T	W		

Temperature (°F) — Normal Time I Measure Temperature: 6:30am

Cycle Day	1	2	3	4	5	6	7	8	9	10	11	12	13	14	15	16	17	18	19	20	21	(22)	23	24	25	26	27	28	29	30	31	32	33	34	35	36	37	38	39	40

Bleeding ● ◒ ○

Mucus	wet / stretchy	damp / gooey	dry / none

Symptoms (physical symptoms, moods, impacts): bloated, back cramps, headache, sore breasts, cramps, acne, acne, sad, tearful, fatigued, craving chocolate, emotional, edgy, bloated

Care (exercises, foods, vitamins, prayers)

Cycle Days 1-2: Arch & Flatten exercise helped pass gas and reduce bloating & back ache

Cycle Days 21-22: Took Vitamin E supplement - may have helped with breast tenderness and cramps compared to last cycle

Cycle Days 30-36: Tried to pray & walk outside in fall leaves each time I felt overwhelmed - seemed to help refocus my thoughts

Note for next cycle: Try to reduce salt in foods to see if helps with bloating

136

Chapter 8 Summary

- Cycle symptoms can be physical and emotional and can occur just prior to your period, during your period, around ovulation, or throughout your entire luteal phase.
    - Charting can help you identify the symptoms you typically experience and when in your cycle they usually occur.

- Natural treatments and care include:
    - Exercising to target specific symptoms
    - Eating healthy foods including vegetables, fruits, whole grains, protein, fat, and water
    - Reducing certain foods like processed foods, caffeine, foods very high in salt, and sugary foods on an empty stomach
    - Choosing foods to minimize additional hormones such as hormone-free beef and dairy
    - Taking vitamins and supplements known to improve cycle health
    - Pampering yourself with home remedies
    - Considering herbal treatments with caution
    - Reducing stress
    - Getting enough sleep
    - Acknowledging your emotions
    - Making time for spiritual reflection
        - Finding beauty in God's creations
        - Praying
        - Admiring other women of faith

- Note the cycle treatments and self-care that work for you in the section labeled "Care" on your chart.

"Do you not know that your body is a temple of the holy Spirit within you, whom you have from God, and that you are not your own? For you have been purchased at a price. Therefore glorify God in your body."
1 Corinthians 6:19

Chapter 9:
The Pill

Perhaps you are wondering, "Isn't it easier to just use birth control pills to regulate my cycle?" While the birth control pill or other hormonal contraceptives may seem like a simple solution to predicting when you will bleed each month and "controlling" your symptoms, they alter the way God designed your body to function naturally, can mask symptoms your body gives you to warn you of other health issues, and can have many side effects in the short term and long term. If the predictability of your cycles is what attracts you to the Pill, you now know that charting your body's own signs can also tell you when your period will start, naturally. If the promise of less bleeding is what attracts you to the Pill, you now know natural and healthy ways that help many people achieve lighter periods as well as reduce other symptoms. Now that you are armed with alternatives, let's look at hormonal contraceptives, how they work, and their potential side effects.

Mechanisms of Hormonal Birth Control

There are several types of hormonal contraceptives. Each functions in a slightly different manner in a woman's body to try to prevent pregnancy. Some hormonal contraceptives also alter or cease a woman's menstrual cycles. For this reason, many medical professionals now prescribe hormonal contraceptives when a girl reports menstrual discomforts or cycle irregularities. While most hormonal contraceptives are used to prevent pregnancy, many young women are also using them for other reasons such as to control or predict bleeding.

Types of Hormonal Contraceptives

The following is a brief overview of the various types of hormonal contraceptives:

- Oral contraceptives, also known as birth control pills or "the Pill", are taken orally every day. Combination pills contain both estrogen and progesterone and progestin-only pills contain only progesterone. Combination pills include monophasic, biphasic, and triphasic pills as well as extended-cycle pills.
- A vaginal ring is a thin, flexible polymer ring which contains both estrogens and progestins. It is inserted into the vagina and left in place for 3 weeks [105].

- A topical patch, also known as a transdermal patch or "the Patch", is a square adhesive patch embedded with both estrogen and progestin. It is placed on the skin somewhere on the body and is typically replaced once a week [106].
- A hormone-embedded IUD (Intra-Uterine Device) is a piece of plastic shaped like a "T" and embedded with progestin. It is inserted into the uterus by a healthcare provider and must be replaced in 3 years [107].
- Implants are thin, flexible plastic rods containing progestin that are surgically placed under the skin of the upper arm. They must be replaced in 3 years [108].
- Injectables are progestin hormones injected into a woman's body as an intramuscular shot, typically every 3 months [109].

Birth control pills are the most commonly used form of hormonal contraceptive, particularly among women ages 15-29 [110] so the following sections focus on the function of these oral contraceptives.

How Oral Contraceptives Alter Your Cycle

Birth control pills typically contain synthetic, or man-made, hormones. The synthetic hormone pills are usually taken for a set number of days and then placebo pills (that do not contain hormones) are taken for a few days. During the time of placebo pills, bleeding typically occurs.

The synthetic hormones in birth control pills interfere with a woman's natural hormones with a primary goal of inhibiting ovulation. In addition, they also change the cervical mucus and prevent the endometrium (lining of the uterus) from building up [9].

Despite popular belief, birth control pills do not "regulate" a girl's cycle. With the additional estrogen and progesterone present in the body from birth control pills, a girl's brain never receives a signal to increase production of FSH and LH. By decreasing levels of FSH and LH, ovulation is suppressed. Without signals from the brain and reproductive hormones to increase production of the four primary hormones at various times, a girl is not actually having a "cycle".

By ingesting additional hormones that interfere with the body's natural production of hormones and then occasionally taking away these synthetic hormones and replacing them with placebos, it produces the outward appearance of a cycle because bleeding occurs at regular intervals. However, the cyclical bleeding while a woman is taking hormonal contraceptives is technically referred to as "withdrawal bleeding" because it usually results from the absence, or withdrawal, of the synthetic hormones. The bleeding is not the result of shedding the lining of the uterus that occurs with a true menstruation. In fact, one of the functions of birth control pills is to prevent the lining of the uterus from building up.

When using certain hormonal contraceptives, irregular bleedings may occur and are sometimes referred to in the medical field as breakthrough bleedings. These irregular bleedings are also not menstruation.

How Oral Contraceptives Prevent Pregnancy

The primary action of birth control pills is to suppress ovulation. If a woman does not ovulate, an egg is not released from the ovaries and cannot be fertilized to create new life. In this action, birth control pills are contraceptive because they prevent conception.

However, birth control pills do not prevent ovulation in all cases [111, 112]. For these instances, the Pill uses other mechanisms to prevent pregnancy. The hormones in birth control pills thicken the cervical mucus (which reduces the likelihood of sperm migration) and reduce Fallopian tube motility (which slows migration of the egg down the tube or sperm up into the tube). In these actions, birth control pills are contraceptive because they prevent the egg and the sperm from uniting (i.e. they prevent conception).

Additionally, the hormones in birth control pills prevent the lining of the uterus (endometrium) from building up so that if ovulation does occur and if an egg is fertilized it will be less likely to implant in the uterus. In this action, and with the belief that life begins at the moment of conception, birth control pills are abortifacient (causing an abortion to occur) because they act after life has been newly conceived to prevent it from further developing, growing, and living in the womb. If a new life is conceived at the moment an egg is fertilized by sperm but the endometrial lining of the uterus is insufficient for the new life to implant, the living child will be shed from the woman's body and die [111].

Although these many functions of birth control pills help to increase their effectiveness in preventing pregnancy, many girls reading this book may not agree morally with both the contraceptive and abortifacient nature of their actions.

Isabella's story

As a teenager, I began taking "the Pill" to regulate my cycles, which seemed extremely unpredictable. When I got married, I continued taking birth control to prevent pregnancy. Many years later, I discovered the mechanisms of how the hormones had been preventing pregnancy and both my husband and I were saddened to wonder if we unknowingly prevented a new life from implanting and growing.

Side Effects

Masking Health Issues

As we have discussed, cycle awareness can help encourage healthier living and reveal potential health issues or medical concerns with your cycle. If you do have an underlying medical issue, taking the Pill will likely not "solve" the medical issue and may only mask the symptoms. Eventually, when you discontinue taking the Pill, the symptoms may return, merely delaying the time until you desire to find a way to live with or treat the symptoms naturally.

Many women discontinue taking the Pill when they desire to try to become pregnant. It may only be at this point that some women learn their body's natural symptoms were a sign of fertility issues. For women with true medical issues such as endometriosis, Polycystic Ovary Syndrome (PCOS), and anovulatory cycles, taking the Pill may only delay treatment of the underlying health concern which may make it more difficult to become pregnant when you eventually desire to conceive a child.

Susanna's story

For the first couple of years of my cycles, my periods were extremely heavy. When I discussed this with my doctor, she told me how the birth control pill would make my bleeding lighter. With no one offering any other suggestions, I decided to take the Pill. I was only 14 years old so by the time I was married and desired to have children, I had been on the Pill for over 10 years. When I stopped taking the Pill, my husband and I tried for many years to become pregnant naturally. We struggled greatly with infertility and finally discovered I had Polycystic Ovary Syndrome (PCOS). All those years on the Pill merely masked the symptoms of PCOS without allowing me to understand or treat the cause. If I, or my doctor, had tried to determine the true cause of my heavy bleeding as a teenager, I feel I would have had a greater chance of treating PCOS and naturally conceiving a child.

Causing Health Problems

If you've ever read the "Prescribing Information" insert inside a prescription of birth control pills, the potential side effects are numerous. You can also find the Prescribing Information for any prescription drug on the internet.

Birth control pills have been shown to increase the risk of serious medical concerns including [9]:

- Myocardial infarction (heart attack)
- Thrombophlebitis and venous thrombosis with or without embolism
- Arterial thromboembolism
- Pulmonary embolism
- Cerebral hemorrhage
- Cerebral thrombosis
- Hypertension
- Gallbladder disease
- Mesenteric thrombosis
- Retinal thrombosis
- Stroke
- Vascular disease (conditions affecting the circulatory system)
- Ocular lesions
- Carbohydrate and lipid metabolic effects
- Hypertriglyceridemia (high levels of triglycerides, associated with cardiovascular disease)
- Decreased glucose tolerance in pre-diabetic and diabetic women
- Elevated blood pressure
- Lipid disorders, including elevated LDL (Low-Density Lipoprotein, i.e. "the bad cholesterol")
- Liver malfunction
- Emotional disorders

Birth control pills can also have adverse reactions including [9]:

- Nausea
- Vomiting
- Gastrointestinal symptoms (such as abdominal cramps and bloating)
- Irregular vaginal bleeding and spotting
- Change in menstrual flow
- Amenorrhea
- Temporary infertility after discontinuation of treatment
- Problems wearing contact lenses such as change in vision or inability to wear contact lenses

144

- Fluid retention
- Edema (swelling), particularly of the fingers or ankles and may raise blood pressure
- Melasma (spotty darkening of the skin), particularly the face, which may persist after discontinuation
- Breast changes: tenderness, enlargement, secretion
- Change in appetite
- Change in weight (increase or decrease)
- Change in cervical erosion and secretion
- Cholestatic jaundice (affecting bowel movements)
- Headaches
- Migraines
- Nervousness
- Mental depression
- Dizziness
- Loss of scalp hair
- Vaginal infections
- Allergic reaction, including rash, urticaria, and angioedema
- Change in corneal curvature
- Hirsutism (excessive hairiness on women on parts of the body where hair does not normally occur or is minimal)
- Acne

Birth control pills may increase the risk of longer term health issues including [9, 112]:
- Breast cancer
- Cervical cancer

Other forms of hormonal birth control (such as the vaginal ring, patch, IUDs, implants, and injectables) have many of the same side effects as oral contraceptives as well as additional side effects based on the form of administration. If you are currently taking any form of hormonal birth control or are considering taking it, please be encouraged to read the full Prescribing Information for the drug and consider the potential side effects.

Interfering with Romantic Relationships

Since hormonal contraceptives work by interfering with our body's natural production of hormones to suppress ovulation, perhaps we should wonder in what other ways suppressing our hormones impacts our lives. Use of hormonal contraceptives influences human brain structure [113]. For a woman who has natural cycles, her fertility can make her naturally more attractive to men [114]. Fertility generally makes a woman more beautiful by making her lips bigger, her pupils dilate, her breasts more symmetrical [115], her voice more attractive [116], her body odor more pleasant [117], and her mood more positive [114]. Fertility also seems to give women an intuition about men and their suitability as potential mates [118]. When using hormonal contraceptives, these natural changes are suppressed. Studies indicate that women using hormonal contraceptives have an increased overall jealousy [119] and are attracted to men with lower testosterone levels [114]. Sexual counselors also warn that birth control may affect long-term relationships [120]. For teen girls and young women who are not sexually active, attractiveness to men is not important from a sexual standpoint. However, as young women date seeking to find their soul mate, they may not want their decisions regarding a potential husband to be clouded by suppressed hormones.

Moral Concerns

Some women have moral or religious concerns with using contraceptives to prevent pregnancy because they alter the natural design and function of a woman's body, can have an abortifacient nature to their actions, and/or prevent giving and receiving love fully the way God intends in marriage. When used solely for medical reasons without the intention of preventing pregnancy, most Christian religions, including Catholicism, do not disapprove of hormonal contraceptives for medical reasons [121, 122].

Using prudence and what you've learned through *Cycles & Spirituality*, it is wise to question if using hormonal contraceptives truly gets to the root of the medical problem you are trying to treat or just masks symptoms; if the benefits of the medication outweigh the risks and side effects; and if taking hormonal contraceptives could weaken your commitment to chastity and God. As with all important decisions, make it with prayerful consideration.

Quitting Birth Control Pills

If you are currently taking birth control pills or another form of hormonal contraceptives and desire to stop taking them, talk with your doctor to discuss the best time to discontinue use. If your doctor is not supportive of your desire to discontinue birth control, you can consider looking for a doctor that is supportive of Natural Family Planning methods (search on www.onemoresoul.com) and therefore fully understands the benefits of having natural cycles the way God intended. If there is not an NFP-supportive doctor in your area, you can continue to see a non-NFP supportive doctor but may want to be prepared to stand firm in your beliefs by making the choice that is right for you. After discontinuing hormonal contraceptives, you can begin using what you've learned in *Cycles & Spirituality* immediately to get to know how your body functions naturally.

Depending on the type of hormonal contraceptives used, it may take a few cycles for your body to return to its normal state. Your body may have to readjust to its own natural hormones. Some girls may experience heavy bleeding for the first cycle after discontinuing the Pill so taking note of the recommendations in this book to reduce PMS and menstrual symptoms (healthy nutrition, exercise, and sleep) will be especially important for the first cycle.

After discontinuing combination birth control pills, about half of girls experience a "normal" cycle the very first cycle. For the other half of girls, cycle impacts may include a short luteal phase (<10 days), no ovulation (no Peak Day or thermal shift on your chart), and long cycles (≥35 days). For some girls, these effects may last for 3-9 months after stopping the pill [123].

After discontinuing progestin-only birth control pills, cycles typically return to "normal" immediately or shortly after discontinuation [112].

After removing the vaginal ring, ovulation typically occurs within 13 days to one month but may take longer in some girls [124, 125].

After removal of a transdermal contraceptive patch, no long-term studies have assessed the length of time for "normal" cycles to return though studies show hormones return to normal levels in about 6 weeks after removing the patch so cycles should most likely resume in this same timeframe [125].

After removing a hormone-embedded IUD, cycles may return to "normal" in 1-3 months [107, 126].

After removing contraceptive implants, ovulation and fertility were reported to return as early as 7 to 14 days after removal [108, 127] and usually within 3 months after removal [125, 128, 129].

After discontinuing injectable contraceptives, the time to return to "normal" cycles is likely to be delayed substantially. After the last shot of injectables, return of ovulation can range between 77-425 days. Depending on the dose of injectables, the average time for return of ovulation is from 7-10 months after the last injection [125, 130]. For some girls, it may take 18 months or longer [109]. During this time, you may follow the steps in *Cycles & Spirituality* to observe and record your signs and help you better understand your returning cycles but your body may not follow a predictable pattern and it may take longer for you to learn your typical luteal phase length and symptoms.

If you make the decision to discontinue using hormonal contraceptives, remember that charting your cycles is not a form of birth control in the manner presented in *Cycles & Spirituality*. This book is designed to help you predict your periods and better understand your overall health. *Cycles & Spirituality* is designed for girls who are not sexually active. If you are engaged or married and are ready to learn Natural Family Planning, an excellent place to build on the knowledge gained through *Cycles & Spirituality* is the Couple to Couple League (www.ccli.org).

Chapter 9 Summary

- For girls who use birth control pills (a.k.a. "the Pill") simply to predict their cycles or to reduce certain symptoms, using *Cycles & Spirituality* may provide a natural way to predict their cycles and manage symptoms without side effects.

- The function of birth control pills is to inhibit ovulation, change cervical mucus, and prevent the lining of the uterus from building up.

- Bleeding while taking the Pill is known as "withdrawal bleeding" and is not true menstruation.

- To prevent pregnancy, the Pill functions as a contraceptive by attempting to prevent an egg from being fertilized and as an abortifacient by attempting to prevent a potentially fertilized egg from implanting in the uterus and continuing to grow.

- The Pill may mask underlying cycle health issues, may increase the risk of serious medical concerns, may have adverse reactions, may increase the risk of longer term health issues, may interfere with romantic relationships, and may raise moral or religious concerns.

- Girls who desire to discontinue the use of hormonal contraceptives should discuss the issue with their doctor.
  - It may take a few cycles for your body to readjust to its own natural hormones.
  - Charting may help you better understand your returning cycles.
  - Charting your cycles is not a form of birth control. *Cycles & Spirituality* is intended for girls who are not sexually active.

Appendix A:
Frequently Asked Questions

Religion

I am not Christian. Can I still use this book to learn about my cycles?

> Yes! Teenage girls and young women of many religious beliefs may benefit from being more in-tune with their bodies and having natural cycles. If you are unsure of your spiritual beliefs or are interested in learning about the Christian faith, perhaps learning about your body and cycles in a spiritual context will provide a new perspective. However, regardless of faith, girls using this book should not be sexually active.

Puberty

I am in the early phases of puberty and have more questions about periods and other changes my body is going through. Is there a specific book you recommend?

> Check out *The Body Book (The Lily Series)* by Nancy Rue. This book is written for tween girls ages 7-11 and discusses the basics of menstruation, breast development, and other changes in a positive way and discusses how becoming a woman is a "God thing" [131].

I have not yet started my first period. Can I use this book to determine when my very first period will begin?

> Perhaps but perhaps not. *Cycles & Spirituality* uses signs of ovulation to predict when menstruation (bleeding following ovulation) will occur. Some girls, particularly those who begin their periods before age 12, may have ovulatory cycles in the first year following menarche. But a girl's first period is not always caused by ovulation and can just be a shedding of the lining of the uterus (known as breakthrough bleeding). If bleeding is not caused by ovulation, the mucus and temperature signs will not show a pattern or allow you to accurately predict when bleeding will occur.

Charting

Can I only chart my temperature (and not my cervical mucus) to predict when my period will occur?

Yes, charting the temperature sign alone will typically give you enough information to determine your thermal shift and luteal phase. Your own individual constant luteal phase length will predict when your next period will occur. However, also charting your cervical mucus will provide a more complete picture of your cycles and better help you understand how the inner workings of your hormones and body may affect how you feel physically and emotionally. If you are only charting your temperature, you will only know when ovulation has occurred (in retrospect) after you observe a sustained rise in temperature. If you are also observing and charting your mucus, you will be able to determine when ovulation is most likely approaching and become more aware of symptoms that may impact your own cycles around that time.

I thought I was in the luteal phase of my cycle but am now having wet/stretchy mucus again. Is my body preparing to ovulate for a second time this cycle? How will this affect when I should expect my period?

If your chart showed a wet/stretchy patch of mucus followed by mucus that was "drying up" *in combination with* a sustained thermal shift, then you should indeed be in the luteal phase of your cycle. Any wet/stretchy mucus observed in the luteal phase is not a sign of another approaching ovulation but is just a normal function of your body. Some girls often see a return of wet/stretchy mucus just prior to their period. Any wet/stretchy mucus observed in the luteal phase will not change when you should expect your next period to start.

My temperatures on my chart are all over the place. I can't find three temperatures above any previous six temperatures and don't seem to have a sustained thermal shift but I still get my period on a regular basis. What does this mean?

If your temperature plot does not show a pattern, first review the best ways to measure your temperature each day. Make sure you are measuring your temperature at approximately the same time each day immediately after waking and before drinking or getting out of bed. Ensure you are placing the thermometer in the proper location, deep under your tongue, and you are keeping your mouth closed the entire time. Also check your thermometer for a low battery. If being more consistent with measuring your temperature still doesn't show a pattern, another possibility is that you may be experiencing anovulatory cycles and breakthrough bleeding. Anovulatory cycles (cycles in which you do not ovulate but the uterus still sheds its lining) can be normal for a few years following menarche (your first period). If you are in your late teen years or in your twenties, consider talking to a doctor knowledgeable of cycle charting to determine if there may be an underlying cause for the lack of a pattern in your temperatures.

I am currently taking birth control pills. Can I chart my cycles for practice while I am still taking the Pill?

While you are welcome to write down your temperature, mucus, and other observations on a chart while you are taking the Pill, the information will not have any significance. It will not provide insight into your physical or emotional symptoms. Most likely you will not see typical mucus patterns or temperature patterns. If you do happen to observe a thermal shift, it will not have any impact on when your withdrawal bleeding will start. To truly understand your body and its signs, begin charting when you have discontinued use of the Pill and are having natural cycles.

Pregnancy Prevention & Sexual Activity

Can I use this book to avoid or achieve a pregnancy (Natural Family Planning)?

No. The information in this book is intended to help you understand your cycles and lays the foundation for using the Sympto-Thermal Method of Natural Family Planning (NFP) but does **not** provide the rules necessary to effectively avoid or achieve a pregnancy. If you are engaged or married, a good source of information for the Sympto-Thermal Method of NFP is the Couple to Couple League (CCL) at www.ccli.org

I am sexually active. Should I still use this book?

While anyone may use this book to better understand their own cycles, the information in this book is not intended to help avoid pregnancy. Simply charting your cycles alone does not prevent conception. For married women who would like to learn how to determine the fertile and infertile phases of their cycle to avoid or achieve pregnancy (known as Natural Family Planning), the Couple to Couple League (CCL) offers instructional courses. For unmarried girls who desire to learn more about God's plan for sexuality, Pope John Paul II's addresses on the Theology of the Body [14] have been condensed into easier-to-study versions such as *Theology of the Body for Teens: Discovering God's Plan for Love and Life* by Brian Butler and Jason and Crystalina Evert [132] and *Theology of the Body for Beginners: A Basic Introduction to Pope John Paul II's Sexual Revolution* by Christopher West [15].

154

Appendix B:
Answers to Practice Charts

Answer # 1

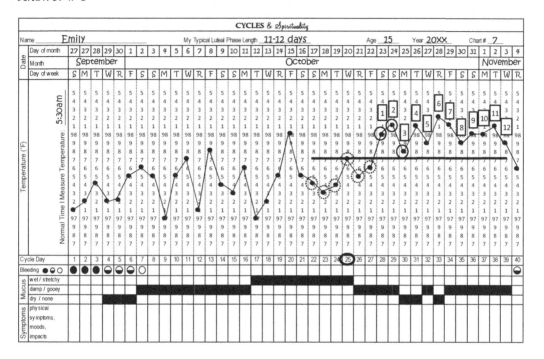

For Emily's chart #7, Peak Day is on cycle day 25 (October 20). The temperatures on cycle days 28, 29, & 30 are higher than the previous six temperatures on cycle days 22-27 and are near Peak Day. The Thermal Shift Line goes through the highest temperature in cycle days 22-27, which is 97.7°F. The luteal phase begins on cycle day 28, the first day her temperature is above the Thermal Shift Line, and lasts until cycle day 39, the day before her period starts. Her luteal phase is 12 days long.

Answer # 2

CYCLES & Spirituality

Name **Emily**   My Typical Luteal Phase Length **11-12 days**   Age **15**   Year **20XX**   Chart # **8a**

Day of month	4	5	6	7	8	9	10	11	12	13	14	15	16	17	18	19	20	21	22	23	24	25	26	27	28	29	30	1	2	3	4	5	6	7	8	9	10	11	12	13
Month												November																				December								

Day of week: R F S S M T W R F S S M T W R F S S M T W R F S S M T W R F S S M T W R F S S M

Temperature (°F) — Normal Time I Measure Temperature: 5:30am

Cycle Day: 1 2 3 4 5 6 7 8 9 10 11 12 13 14 15 16 17 18 19 20 21 22 23 24 25 26 27 28 29 (30) 31 32 33 34 35 36 37 38 39 40

Bleeding ●○○

Mucus: wet/stretchy, damp/gooey, dry/none

Symptoms: physical symptoms, moods, impacts

For Emily's chart #8, Peak Day is on cycle day 30 (December 3). The temperatures on cycle days 32, 33, & 34 are higher than the previous six temperatures on cycle days 26-31 and are near Peak Day. The Thermal Shift Line goes through the highest temperature in cycle days 26-31, which is 97.8°F. The luteal phase begins on cycle day 32. Her typical luteal phase length is 11-12 days. Counting 11-12 days from cycle day 32, Emily should expect her luteal phase to last until around cycle day 42-43 (December 15-16) and should expect her period to start on cycle day 43-44. Since luteal phase length can vary slightly, Emily should not be terribly surprised if her period begins somewhere between cycle days 42-45. Since this cycle will be longer than 40 days, Emily will need to start a new chart. Notice she numbered the first chart "8a" and will number the next chart "8b" to denote it as a continuation of the previous.

Name _____ Emily _____ My Typical Luteal Phase Length **11-12 days** Age __15__ Year **20XX** Chart # **8b**

Date	Day of month	14	15	16																																				
	Month	December																																							
	Day of week	T	W	R																																				

Temperature (°F)

Normal Time I Measure Temperature: 5:30am

(Temperature grid with values 10, 11, 12 entered in first three columns; remaining columns pre-printed with scale 5,4,3,2,1 / 98,9,8,7,6,5,4,3,2,1 / 97,9,8,7)

Cycle Day	1	2	3	4	5	6	7	8	9	10	11	12	13	14	15	16	17	18	19	20	21	22	23	24	25	26	27	28	29	30	31	32	33	34	35	36	37	38	39	40
Bleeding ●◐○																																								
Mucus — wet / stretchy																																								
Mucus — damp / gooey																																								
Mucus — dry / none																																								
Symptoms — physical symptoms, moods, impacts																																								

157

Answer # 3

CYCLES & Spirituality

Name __Madison__   My Typical Luteal Phase Length __13-14 days__   Age __19__   Year __20XX__   Chart # __13__

Month: November

Day of month: 1 2 3 4 5 6 7 8 9 10 11 12 13 14 15 16 17 18 19 20 21 22 23 24 25 26 27 28 29 30

Temperature (°F) — Normal Time I Measure Temperature: 7:00am

Cycle Day: 1 2 3 4 5 6 7 8 9 10 11 12 13 14 15 16 17 (18) 19 20 21 22 23 24 25 26 27 28 29 30 31 32 33 34 35 36 37 38 39 40

Bleeding ● ○

Mucus: wet / stretchy — damp / gooey — dry / none

Symptoms: physical symptoms, moods, impacts — sad & bloated — emotional & crampy — fatigued — not enough sleep — happy — bloated — moody & gassy

For Madison's chart #13, Peak Day is on cycle day 18 (November 18). Notice she waited for three days of mucus that was "drying up" (not wet/stretchy) before labeling Peak Day. The temperatures on cycle days 17, 18, & 19 are higher than the previous six temperatures on cycle days 11-16 and are near Peak Day. The Thermal Shift Line goes through the highest temperature in cycle days 11-16, which is 97.9°F. The luteal phase begins on cycle day 17. Her typical luteal phase length is 13-14 days. Counting 13-14 days from cycle day 17, Madison should expect her luteal phase to last until around cycle day 29-30 (November 29-30) and her period to start around cycle day 30-31 (November 30-December 1). Since luteal phase length can vary slightly, Madison should not be terribly surprised if her period begins somewhere between cycle days 29-32.

158

Appendix C: Blank Chart

CYCLES & *Spirituality*

Name _____ Age _____ Year _____ Chart # _____

My Typical Luteal Phase Length _____

Normal Time | Measure Temperature: _____

Date	
Day of month	
Month	
Day of week	

Temperature (°F)

Cycle Day: 1 2 3 4 5 6 7 8 9 10 11 12 13 14 15 16 17 18 19 20 21 22 23 24 25 26 27 28 29 30 31 32 33 34 35 36 37 38 39 40

Bleeding	○ ◑ ●
Mucus	wet / stretchy
	damp / gooey
	dry / none
Symptoms	physical symptoms, moods, impacts
Care	exercises, foods, vitamins, prayers

159

Glossary

Abstinence – refraining from sexual intercourse

Abortifacient – an agent (device or chemical) that causes an abortion. Abortifacients may act by removing a growing fetus from the womb or by preventing a newly fertilized egg from implanting in the uterus

Amenorrhea – the absence or cessation of menstruation

Anovulatory cycle – a cycle in which ovulation does not occur

Basal body temperature – the lowest temperature your body achieves during rest, usually measured immediately after awakening from sleep in the morning

Basal body thermometer – a thermometer with increased accuracy in the typical range of basal body temperatures

Birth control pill – hormonal contraceptive pills taken orally

Breakthrough bleeding – vaginal bleeding that occurs to shed the built-up endometrium, even though ovulation did not take place

Cervical mucus – a natural and healthy fluid produced by the cervix in response to hormones

Cervix – an internal organ near the opening of the vagina that helps protect a growing baby

Chastity – a moral virtue, the act of living a sexually pure life

Clitoris – the sensitive and erectile external organ of the vagina

Endometriosis – the growth of endometrial glands outside of the lining of the uterus, such as on the ovaries, behind the uterus, on the bowels, on the bladder, or rarely in other parts of the body

Endometrium – the lining of the uterus

Estrogen – a hormone produced in the female reproductive organs that prepares the uterus, cervix, and cervical mucus to potentially aid in fertilizing an egg and allowing the newly conceived life to implant in the uterus

Fallopian tubes – two tubes leading from the ovaries to the uterus used to transport eggs

Follicle Stimulating Hormone (FSH) – a hormone produced in the brain that signals the ovaries to mature an egg

Follicular phase – the phase of the menstrual cycle during which the lining of the uterus (endometrium) builds up and the ovaries prepare an egg

Hormonal contraceptives – medications or devices that contain hormones intended to alter the natural female reproductive cycle by preventing ovulation and/or preventing implantation of a fertilized egg to prevent conception/pregnancy

Hormones – chemical messengers produced in one part of the body and transported by the bloodstream to another part of the body to bring about physiological activity

Hypothyroidism – an endocrine disorder in which the thyroid gland is underactive

Intra-Uterine Device (IUD) – a piece of plastic shaped like a "T" (usually embedded with hormones) that is inserted into the uterus to prevent conception/pregnancy

Labia – the folds of skin surrounding the opening of the vagina

Luteal phase – the phase of the menstrual cycle from ovulation to the start of menstruation

Luteinizing Hormone (LH) – a hormone produced in the brain that signals ovulation to occur

Menarche – a girl's first menstrual period

Menorrhagia – excessive uterine bleeding

Menstrual cycle – the cycle of the female reproductive system caused by hormones. It begins with menstruation and continues with the follicular phase, ovulation, and the luteal phase.

Menstruation – bleeding caused by the shedding of the lining of the uterus (the endometrium) approximately 2 weeks after ovulation.

Mittelschmerz – ovulation pain; from the German words for "middle" and "pain"

Natural Family Planning (NFP) – observing and understanding a woman's fertility signs to determine the fertile and infertile phases of her cycle; this knowledge can then be used to either postpone pregnancy or help achieve pregnancy

Ovaries – the two internal female reproductive organs that produce eggs

Ovulation – the release of an egg from the ovaries

Ovulatory cycle – a menstrual cycle in which ovulation occurs

Ovum – the mature egg released during ovulation

Peak Day – the last day of wet/stretchy mucus with at least three days of mucus that is "drying up" following it

Pill – a commonly used name for birth control pills

Polycystic Ovary Syndrome (PCOS) – an endocrine system disorder usually associated with enlarged ovaries that contain small collections of fluid

PreMenstrual Syndrome (PMS) – emotional and physical symptoms associated with the time prior to and at the beginning of menstruation in the female reproductive cycle

Progesterone – a hormone produced in the female reproductive organs that signals the glands in the cervix to thicken, dry up, or stop producing cervical mucus; signals the cervix to close and harden; continues to enrich the endometrium; and causes the basal body temperature to rise

Thermal shift – a rise in waking basal body temperature, usually by about 0.4°F, around the time of ovulation

Thermal Shift Line – a visual aid to help identify the thermal shift on your chart; a horizontal line drawn through the highest temperature in the six temperatures that precede the thermal shift

Thyroid – an endocrine gland found in the neck

Uterus – the internal female reproductive organ, also known as the "womb", where a fertilized egg can implant to grow into a baby

Vagina – the canal that extends from the cervix to the vaginal opening at the labia and clitoris

Vulva – the external female parts that include the labia and clitoris

Withdrawal bleeding – bleeding experienced while taking hormonal contraceptives

References

[1]   G. Martinez, C. Copen and J. Abma, "Teenagers in the United States: Sexual Activity, Contraceptive Use, and Childbearing, 2006-2010 National Survey of Family Growth," *Vital and Health Statistics,* vol. 23, no. 31, 2011.

[2]   Ø. Lindegaard, E. Løkkegaard, A. Jensen, C. Skovlund and N. Keiding, "Thrombotic Stroke and Myocardial Infarction with Hormonal Contraception," *The New England Journal of Medicine,* vol. 366, pp. 2257-2266, 2012.

[3]   "FDA Drug Safety Communication: Updated information about the risk of blood clots in women taking birth control pills containing drospirenone," U.S. Food and Drug Administration, 2013. [Online]. Available: http://www.fda.gov/Drugs/DrugSafety/ucm299305.htm. [Accessed 18 Feb 2015].

[4]   D. Scholes, L. Ichikawa, A. LaCroix, L. Spangler, J. Beasley, S. Reed and S. Ott, "Oral Contraceptive Use and Bone Density Change in Adolescent and Young Adult Women: A Prospective Study of Age, Hormone Dose, and Discontinuation," *The Journal of Clinical Endocrinology and Metabolism,* vol. 96, no. 9, pp. E1380-E1387, 2011.

[5]   "Safety: Depo-Provera," U.S. Food and Drug Administration, 2013. [Online]. Available: http://www.fda.gov/Safety/MedWatch/SafetyInformation/SafetyAlertsforHumanMedicalP roducts/ucm154784.htm. [Accessed 18 Feb 2015].

[6]   "Fact Sheet: Oral Contraceptives and Cancer Risk," National Cancer Institute at the National Institutes of Health, 2012. [Online]. Available: http://www.cancer.gov/cancertopics/factsheet/Risk/oral-contraceptives. [Accessed 18 Feb 2015].

[7]   "Table 9: Birth control pills and breast cancer risk," Susan G. Komen, 2014. [Online]. Available: http://ww5.komen.org/BreastCancer/Table9Birthcontrolpillsandbreastcancerrisk.html#sth ash.V0wNHbO2.dpuf. [Accessed 18 Feb 2015].

[8]   H. Nelson, B. Zakher, A. Cantor, R. Fu, J. Griffin, E. O'Meara, D. Buist, K. Kerlikowske, N. van Ravesteyn, A. Trentham-Dietz, J. Mandelblatt and D. Miglioretti, "Risk factors for breast cancer for women aged 40 to 49 years: a systematic review and meta-analysis," *Annals of Internal Medicine,* vol. 156, no. 9, pp. 635-648, 2012.

[9]   "Prescribing information: Ortho-Tri-Cyclen-Lo," Janssen Pharmaceuticals, Inc., 2014. [Online]. Available: https://thepill.com/sites/default/files/pdf/Tri-Cyclen_Lo_PI.pdf#zoom=100. [Accessed 18 Feb 2015].

[10]   M. A. Wilson, "The Practice of Natural Family Planning versus the use of Artificial Birth Control: Family, Sexual and Moral Issues," *Catholic Social Science Review,* vol. VII, 2002.

[11]   A.-M. Ambert, "Cohabitation and Marriage: How are they related," *Contemporary Family Trends: The Vanier Institute of the Family,* 2005.

[12]   Frank-Herrmann, P., J. Heil, C. Gnoth, E. Toledo, S. Baur, C. Pyper, E. Jenetzky, T. Strowitzki and G. Freundl, "The effectiveness of a fertility awareness based method to avoid pregnancy in relation to a couple's sexual behaviour during the fertile time: a prospective longitudinal study," *Human Reproduction,* vol. 22, no. 5, pp. 1310-1319, 2007.

[13]   New American Bible, revised edition, Washington, D.C.: Confraternity of Christian Doctrine, 2010.

[14]   Pope John Paul II, "General Audiences: John Paul II's Theology of the Body," EWTN.com, 1979-1984.

[15]   C. West, Theology of the Body for Beginners: A Basic Introduction to Pope John Paul II's Sexual Revolution, Revised Edition, West Chester: Ascension Press, 2009.

[16]   The Couple to Couple League International, Inc., The Art of Natural Family Planning Student Guide, Second Edition, Cincinnati: The Couple to Couple League International, Inc., 2011.

[17]   S. J. Emans, M. Laufer and D. Goldstein, Pediatric & Adolescent Gynecology, Fifth Edition, Philadelphia: Lippincott Williams & Wilkins, 2005.

[18]   ACOG Committee on Adolescent Health Care: American Academy of Pediatrics Committee on Adolescence, "Menstruation in Girls and Adolescents: Using the Menstrual Cycle as a Vital Sign (Committee Opinion 349)," The American College of Obstetricians and Gynecologists, Washington D.C., 2006.

[19]   Pope Paul VI Institute For the Study of Human Reproduction, "The Real Main Event of Your Menstrual Cycle," Fertility Care for Young Women: A Newsletter Dedicated to Helping Women Appreciate Their Fertility, no. 1, 2009.

[20]   J. S. Berek, Berek & Novak's Gynecology, Fourteenth Edition, Philadelphia: Lippincott Williams & Wilkins, 2007.

[21]   R. Hatcher, J. Trussell, A. Nelson, W. Cates, Jr. and F. Stewart, Contraceptive Technology, 19th Edition, New York: Ardent Media, 2007.

[22]   V. Braun, "NFP primer for learning couples," Family Foundations, Jan/Feb 2015.

[23]   E. Odeblad, "The Discovery of Different Types of Cervical Mucus and the Billings Ovulation Method," Bulletin of the Ovulation Method Research and Reference Centre of Australia, vol. 21, no. 3, pp. 3-25, 1994.

[24]   V. Braun, "Fertility awareness and the unmarried," Family Foundations, pp. 36-37, Mar/Apr 2014.

[25]   "Body Mass Index Table 1," National Institutes of Health: National Heart, Lung, and Blood Institute, [Online]. Available: http://www.nhlbi.nih.gov/health/educational/lose_wt/BMI/bmi_tbl.htm. [Accessed 18 Feb 2015].

[26]   "Calculate Your Body Mass Index Table 1," National Institutes of Health: National Heart, Lung, and Blood Institute, [Online]. Available: http://www.nhlbi.nih.gov/health/educational/lose_wt/BMI/bmicalc.htm. [Accessed 18 Feb 2015].

[27]   M. Shannon, Fertility, Cycles, & Nutrition, 4th Edition, Cincinnati: The Couple to Couple League International, Inc., 2009.

[28]   M. De Souza, "Menstrual Disturbances in Athletes: A Focus on Luteal Phase Defects," Medicine & Science in Sports & Exercise, vol. 35, no. 9, pp. 1553-1563, 2003.

[29]   Mayo Clinic Staff, "Diseases and Conditions: Yeast infection (vaginal)," Mayo Clinic, 2012. [Online]. Available: http://www.mayoclinic.org/diseases-conditions/yeast-infection/basics/definition/CON-20035129?p=1. [Accessed 18 Feb 2015].

[30] "Hypothyroidism," Medline Plus, U.S National Library of Medicine, National Institutes of Health, 2015. [Online]. Available: http://www.nlm.nih.gov/medlineplus/hypothyroidism.html. [Accessed 18 Feb 2015].

[31] Mayo Clinic Staff, "Diseases and conditions: Polycystic ovary syndrome (PCOS)," Mayo Clinic, 2014. [Online]. Available: http://www.mayoclinic.org/diseases-conditions/pcos/basics/definition/con-20028841. [Accessed 18 Feb 2015].

[32] "Benadryl Side Effects Center," RxList, 2015. [Online]. Available: http://www.rxlist.com/benadryl-side-effects-drug-center.htm. [Accessed 18 Feb 2015].

[33] "Paxil," RxList, 2015. [Online]. Available: http://www.rxlist.com/paxil-drug/side-effects-interactions.htm. [Accessed 18 Feb 2015].

[34] "Imodium," RxList, 2015. [Online]. Available: http://www.rxlist.com/imodium-drug/side-effects-interactions.htm. [Accessed 18 Feb 2015].

[35] "Naprosyn, Anaprox, Anaprox DS," RxList, 2015. [Online]. Available: http://www.rxlist.com/naprosyn-drug/side-effects-interactions.htm. [Accessed 18 Feb 2015].

[36] "Deltasone Side Effects Center," RxList, 2015. [Online]. Available: http://www.rxlist.com/deltasone-side-effects-drug-center.htm. [Accessed 18 Feb 2015].

[37] "Dramamine Side Effects," Drugs.com, 2015. [Online]. Available: http://www.drugs.com/sfx/dramamine-side-effects.html. [Accessed 18 Feb 2015].

[38] "Guaifenesin," Drugs.com, 2015. [Online]. Available: http://www.drugs.com/guaifenesin.html. [Accessed 18 Feb 2015].

[39] "Premenstrual Breast Changes," Medline Plus, U.S National Library of Medicine, National Institutes of Health, 2015. [Online]. Available: http://www.nlm.nih.gov/medlineplus/ency/article/003153.htm. [Accessed 18 Feb 2015].

[40] "Migraines, Headaches, and Hormones," WebMD, 2015. [Online]. Available: http://www.webmd.com/migraines-headaches/guide/hormones-headaches. [Accessed 18 Feb 2015].

[41] "Blood Disorders in Women: Heavy Menstrual Bleeding," Centers for Disease Control and Prevention, 2014. [Online]. Available: http://www.cdc.gov/ncbddd/blooddisorders/women/menorrhagia.html. [Accessed 18 Feb 2015].

[42] "Premenstrual syndrome," American College of Obstetricians and Gynecologists, 2011. [Online]. Available: http://www.acog.org/publications/faq/faq057.cfm. [Accessed 18 Feb 2015].

[43] B. Bauer, Mayo Clinic Book of Alternative Medicine, New York: Time Inc. Home Entertainment, 2007.

[44] V. Stooke, Interviewee, *Director, Form Studio*. [Interview]. 9 Feb 2015.

[45] L. Gates, "Somatic Sequence for Relieving Lower Back Pain," Somatic Education in the Tradition of Thomas Hanna, [Online]. Available: http://www.fullmovementpotential.com/somatic-sequences/. [Accessed 18 Feb 2015].

[46] H. Zhang, M. Zhu, Y. Song and M. Kong, "Baduanjin exercise improved premenstrual syndrome symptoms in Macau women," *Journal of Traditional Chinese Medicine,* vol. 34, no. 4, pp. 460-464, 2014.

[47]   Mayo Clinic Staff, "Diseases and conditions: Pre-Menstrual Syndrome (PMS)," Mayo Clinic, 2012. [Online]. Available: http://www.mayoclinic.org/diseases-conditions/premenstrual-syndrome/basics/definition /CON-20020003. [Accessed 18 Feb 2015].

[48]   A. Fjerbaek and U. Knudsen, "Endometriosis, dysmenorrhea and diet--what is the evidence?: Abstract," *European Journal of Obstetrics, Gynecology, and Reproductive Biology,* vol. 132, no. 2, pp. 140-147, 2007.

[49]   Mayo Clinic Staff, "Dietary fats: Know which types to choose," Mayo Clinic Healthy Lifestyle: Nutrition and healthy eating, 7 August 2014. [Online]. Available: http://www.mayoclinic.org/healthy-lifestyle/nutrition-and-healthy-eating/in-depth/fat/art-20045550. [Accessed 18 November 2015].

[50]   M. Grootveld, C. Silwood, P. Addis, A. Claxson, B. Bonet Serra and M. Viana, "Health Effects of Oxidized Heated Oils - Abstract," *Foodservice Research International,* vol. 13, no. 1, pp. 41-55, 2001.

[51]   K. Gunnars, "Healthy Cooking Oils - The Ultimate Guide," Authority Nutrition, May 2013. [Online]. Available: http://authoritynutrition.com/healthy-cooking-oils/. [Accessed 18 November 2015].

[52]   A. Paturel, "Boost Brain Power with GOod Fats," Cleveland Clinic Wellness, 8 September 2009. [Online]. Available: http://www.clevelandclinicwellness.com/food/GoodFats/Pages/BoostBrainPowerwithGoodFats.aspx#. [Accessed 18 November 2015].

[53]   M. Oz, "Daily Dose: Omega-3," The Dr. Oz Show, 3 June 2010. [Online]. Available: http://www.doctoroz.com/article/daily-dose-omega-3. [Accessed 18 Novemeber 2015].

[54]   R. Patterson, S. Flatt, V. Newman, L. Natarajan, C. Rock, C. Thomson, B. Caan, B. Parker and J. Pierce, "Marine Fatty Acid Intake is Associated with Breast Cancer Prognosis," *The Journal of Nutrition,* vol. 141, no. 2, pp. 201-206, 2011.

[55]   University of Maryland Medical Center, "Omega-3 fatty acids," University of Maryland Medical Center, 2015. [Online]. Available: http://umm.edu/health/medical/altmed/supplement/omega3-fatty-acids/. [Accessed 18 November 2015].

[56]   Z. Harel, F. Biro, R. Kottenhahn and S. Rosenthanl, "Supplementation with omega-3 polyunsaturated fatty acids in the management of dysmenorrhea in adolescents - Abstract," *American Journal of Obstetrics & Gynecology,* vol. 174, no. 4, pp. 1335-1338, 1996.

[57]   A. Nadjarzadeh, R. D. Firouzabadi, N. Vaziri, H. Daneshbodi, M. H. Lotfi and H. Mozaffari-Khosravi, "The effect of omega-3 supplementation on androgen profile and menstrual status in women with polycystic ovary syndrome: A randomized clinical trial," *Iran Journal of Reproductive Medicine,* vol. 11, no. 8, pp. 665-672, 2013.

[58]   University of Maryland Medical Center, "Omega-6 fatty acids," University of Maryland Medical Center, 2013. [Online]. Available: http://umm.edu/health/medical/altmed/supplement/omega6-fatty-acids. [Accessed 18 November 2015].

[59]   M. de Lorgeril and P. Salen, "New insights into the health effects of dietary saturated and omega-6 and omega-3 polyunsaturated fatty acids," *BMC Medicine,* vol. 10, no. 50, 2012.

168

[60] N. Teicholz, "The Questionable Link Between Saturated Fat and Heart Disease," The Wall Street Journal, 6 May 2014. [Online]. Available: http://www.wsj.com/articles/SB10001424052702303678404579533760760481486. [Accessed 18 November 2015].

[61] P. Siri-Tarino, Q. Sun, F. Hu and R. Krauss, "Saturated fat, carbohydrate, and cardiovascular disease," *American Journal of Clinical Nutrition,* vol. 91, no. 3, pp. 502-509, 2010.

[62] D. Mozaffarian, E. Rimm and D. Herrington, "Dietary fats, carbohydrate, and progression or coronary atherosclerosis in postmenopausal women," *American Journal of Clinical Nutrition,* vol. 80, pp. 1175-84, 2004.

[63] J. Chavarro, J. Rich-Edwards, B. Rosner and W. Willett, "A prospective study of dairy foods intake and anovulatory infertility," *Human Reproduction,* vol. 22, no. 5, pp. 1340-1347, 2007.

[64] E. Bertone-Johnson, S. Hankinson, A. Bendich, S. Johnson, W. Willett and J. Manson, "Calcium and Vitamin D Intake and Risk of Incident Premenstrual Syndrome," *JAMA Internal Medicine,* vol. 165, no. 11, pp. 1246-1252, 2005.

[65] P. LoGiudice, S. Bleakney and P. Bongiorno, "The Surprising Health Benefits of Coconut Oil," The Dr. Oz Show, 29 October 2012. [Online]. Available: http://www.doctoroz.com/article/surprising-health-benefits-coconut-oil. [Accessed 18 November 2015].

[66] K. Gunnars, "Why is Coconut Oil Good For You? The Healthiest Oil for Cooking," Authority Nutrition, March 2013. [Online]. Available: http://authoritynutrition.com/why-is-coconut-oil-good-for-you/. [Accessed 18 November 2015].

[67] "Questions and Answers Regarding Trans Fat," U.S. Food and Drug Administration, 2014. [Online]. Available: www.fda.gov/Food/PopularTopics/ucm373922.htm. [Accessed 18 Feb 2015].

[68] M. Tedstrom and L. Wilson, "Menstrual Hypoglycemia and Functional Dysmenorrhea: Their Relationship," *Western Journal of Medicine,* vol. 44, no. 5, pp. 375-381, 1936.

[69] Q. Yang, Z. Zhang, E. Gregg, W. D. Flanders, R. Merritt and F. Hu, "Added Sugar Intake and Cardiovascular Diseases Mortality Among US Adults," *JAMA Internal Medicine,* vol. 174, no. 4, pp. 516-524, 2014.

[70] G. Fagherazzi, A. Vilier, D. S. Sartorelli, M. Lajous, B. Balkau and . F. Clavel-Chapelon, "Consumption of artificially and sugar-sweetened beverages and incident type 2 diabetes in the Etude Epidémiologique auprès des femmes de la Mutuelle Générale de l'Education Nationale–European Prospective Investigation into Cancer and Nutrition cohort," *American Journal of Clinical Nutrition,* vol. doi: 10.3945/ajcn.112.050997 , 2013.

[71] A. Rossignol and H. Bonnlander, "Caffeine-containing beverages, total fluid consumption, and premenstrual syndrome," *American Journal of Public Health,* vol. 80, no. 9, pp. 1106-1110, 1990.

[72] "Midol Complete Caplets Drug Facts," Bayer HealthCare Consumer Care, 2014. [Online]. Available: http://www.midol.com/static/documents/WEB_Midol-Complete-Caplets-011.pdf. [Accessed 20 May 2015].

[73]   "Sodium in Diet," Medline Plus, U.S National Library of Medicine, National Institutes of Health, 2015. [Online]. Available: www.nlm.nih.gov/medlineplus/ency/article/002415.htm. [Accessed 18 Feb 2015].

[74]   G. Abraham, "Nutritional factors in the etiology of the premenstrual tension syndromes: Abstract," *Journal of Reproductive Medicine,* vol. 28, no. 7, pp. 446-464, 1983.

[75]   P. Chocano-Bedoya, J. Manson, S. Hankinson, W. Willett, S. Johnson, L. Chasan-Taber, A. Ronnenberg, C. Bigelow and E. Bertone-Johnson, "Dietary B vitamin intake and incident premenstrual syndrome," *The American Journal of Clinical Nutrition,* vol. doi: 10.3945/ajcn.110.009530, 2011.

[76]   P. Chocano-Bedoya, J. Manson, S. Hankinson, S. Johnson, L. Chasan-Taber, A. Ronnenberg, C. Bigelow and E. Bertone-Johnson, "Intake of Selected Minerals and Risk of Premenstrual Syndrome," *American Journal of Epidemiology,* vol. 177, no. 10, pp. 1118-1127, 2012.

[77]   A. Livdans-Forret, P. Harvey and S. Larkin-Their, "Menorrhagia: a synopsis of management focusing on herbal and nutritional supplements, and chiropractic," *The Journal of the Canadian Chiropractic Association,* vol. 51, no. 4, pp. 235-246, 2007.

[78]   "Vitamin C: Fact Sheet for Health Professionals," National Institutes of Health, Office of Dietary Supplements, 5 June 2013. [Online]. Available: https://ods.od.nih.gov/factsheets/VitaminC-HealthProfessional/. [Accessed 18 November 2015].

[79]   "EWG's 2014 Shopper's Guide to Pesticides in Produce™," Ewg.org. Environmental Working Group, 2014. [Online]. Available: http://www.ewg.org/foodnews/. [Accessed 18 Feb 2015].

[80]   "Steroid Hormone Implants Used for Growth in Food-Producing Animals," U.S. Food and Drug Administration, Animal & Veterinary, 2014. [Online]. Available: http://www.fda.gov/AnimalVeterinary/SafetyHealth/ProductSafetyInformation/ucm055436.htm. [Accessed 18 Feb 2015].

[81]   S. Epstein, "Hormones in U.S. Beef," Huffpost Healthy Living. The Huffington Post, 2011. [Online]. Available: http://www.huffingtonpost.com/samuel-s-epstein/hormones-in-us-beef_b_325784.html. [Accessed 18 Feb 2015].

[82]   S. Epstein, "A Ban on Hormonal Meat Is 30 Years Overdue," Huffpost Healthy Living. The Huffington Post, 2011. [Online]. Available: http://www.huffingtonpost.com/samuel-s-epstein/a-ban-on-hormonal-meat-is_b_446060.html. [Accessed 18 Feb 2015].

[83]   "Report on the Food and Drug Administration's Review of the Safety of Recombinant Bovine Somatotropin," U.S. Food and Drug Administration, Animal & Veterinary, 2014. [Online]. Available: http://www.fda.gov/AnimalVeterinary/SafetyHealth/ProductSafetyInformation/ucm130321.htm#top. [Accessed 18 Feb 2015].

[84]   "rBGH," Sustainabletable.org, GRACE Communications Foundation, 2015. [Online]. Available: http://www.sustainabletable.org/797/rbgh. [Accessed 18 Feb 2015].

[85]   J. Mercola, "The Health Dangers of Soy," HuffPost Healthy Living, TheHuffingtonPost.com, Inc, 2012. [Online]. Available: http://www.huffingtonpost.com/dr-mercola/soy-health_b_1822466.html. [Accessed 20 May 2015].

[86]   M. Shannon, "Supplements to Consider for Specific Problems," *Family Foundations,* pp. 30-31, Mar/Apr 2014.

[87]   Mayo Clinic Staff, "Diseases and conditions: Pre-Menstrual Syndrome (PMS): Alternative Medicine," Mayo Clinic, 2014. [Online]. Available: http://www.mayoclinic.org/diseases-conditions/premenstrual-syndrome/basics/alternative-medicine/con-20020003?reDate=13012015. [Accessed 18 Feb 2015].

[88]   "Premenstrual syndrome (PMS) fact sheet," Womenshealth.gov. Office on Women's Health, U.S. Department of Health and Human Services, 2014. [Online]. Available: http://www.womenshealth.gov/publications/our-publications/fact-sheet/premenstrual-syndrome.html. [Accessed 18 Feb 2015].

[89]   M. Proctor and P. Murphy, "Herbal and dietary therapies for primary and secondary dysmenorrhea: Abstract," *Cochrane Database of Systematic Reviews, John Wiley & Sons, Ltd,* 2001.

[90]   M. Sircus, "Magnesium and Chocolate Therapy for Heart Disease and Stroke," Dr.Sircus.com, 2010. [Online]. Available: http://drsircus.com/medicine/magnesium/magnesium-chocolate-therapy-heart-disease-stroke/. [Accessed 18 Feb 2015].

[91]   S. Ziaei, M. Zakeri and A. Kazemnejad, "A randomised controlled trial of vitamin E in the treatment of primary dysmenorrhea," *BJOG: An International Journal fo Obstetrics & Gynaecology,* vol. 112, no. 4, pp. 466-469, 2005.

[92]   D. Lithgow and W. Politzer, "Vitamin A in the treatment of menorrhagia," *South African Medical Journal,* vol. 51, no. 7, pp. 191-193, 1977.

[93]   K. Wyatt, P. Dimmock, P. Jones and P. O'Brien, "Efficacy of vitamin B-6 in the treatment of premenstrual syndrome: systematic review," *BMJ,* vol. 318, pp. 1375-1381, 1999.

[94]   Z. Harel, F. Biro, R. Kottenhahn and S. Rosenthal, "Supplementation with omega-3 poly-unsaturated fatty acids in the management of dysmenorrhea in adolescents: Abstract," *American Journal of Obstetrics & Gynecology,* vol. 174, no. 4, pp. 1335-1338, 1996.

[95]   W. Phipps, M. Martini, J. Lampe, J. Slavin and M. Kurzer, "Effect of flax seed ingestion on the menstrual cycle," *Journal of Clinical Endocrinology & Metabolism,* vol. 77, no. 5, pp. 1215-1219, 1993.

[96]   E. Rocha Filho, J. Lima, J. Pinho Neto and U. Montarroyos, "Essential fatty acids for premenstrual syndrome and their effect on prolactin and total cholesterol levels: a randomized, double blind, placebo-controlled study," *Reproductive Health,* vol. 8, no. 2, 2011.

[97]   R. Waring, "Report on Absorption of magnesium sulfate (Epsom salts) across the skin," Epsom Salt Council, [Online]. Available: http://www.epsomsaltcouncil.org/articles/report_on_absorption_of_magnesium_sulfate.pdf. [Accessed 11 November 2015].

[98]   "6 Herbs for PMS," U by Kotex, Kimberly-Clark Corporation, [Online]. Available: www.kotex.com/na/articles-info/6-herbs-for-pms/10205. [Accessed 25 Mar 2015].

[99]   "Chasteberry," National Institutes of Health, National Center for Complementary and Integrative Health, 2012. [Online]. Available: http://nccam.nih.gov/health/chasteberry. [Accessed 18 Feb 2015].

[100] "Raspberry Leaf," Traditional Medicinals, [Online]. Available: www.traditionalmedicinals.com/products/raspberry-leaf/. [Accessed 25 Mar 2015].

[101] "Black Cohosh," National Institutes of Health, National Center for Complementary and Integrative Health, 2012. [Online]. Available: http://nccam.nih.gov/health/blackcohosh/ataglance.htm. [Accessed 18 Feb 2015].

[102] "Evening Primrose Oil," National Institutes of Health, National Center for Complementary and Integrative Health, 2013. [Online]. Available: http://nccam.nih.gov/health/eveningprimrose. [Accessed 18 Feb 2015].

[103] "Health Care for College Students," Healthychildren.org. American Academy of Pediatrics, 2015. [Online]. Available: http://www.healthychildren.org/English/ages-stages/young-adult/Pages/Health-Care-for-College-Students.aspx. [Accessed 18 Feb 2015].

[104] M. Shannon, "Proactive strategies for better cycles for our daughters," *Family Foundations*, pp. 28-29, Mar/Apr 2014.

[105] "Patient Information: NuvaRing," Merck & Co. Inc, 2012. [Online]. Available: http://www.merck.com/product/usa/pi_circulars/n/nuvaring/nuvaring_pi.pdf. [Accessed 18 Feb 2015].

[106] "Patient Information: Ortho Evra," Janssen Pharmaceuticals, Inc., 2014. [Online]. Available: http://www.orthoevra.com/sites/default/files/assets/OrthoEvraPI.pdf. [Accessed 18 Feb 2015].

[107] "Patient Information: Skyla," Bayer HealthCare Pharmaceuticals, 2013. [Online]. Available: http://labeling.bayerhealthcare.com/html/products/pi/Skyla_PI.pdf. [Accessed 18 Feb 2015].

[108] "Patient Information: Implanon," Merck & Co. Inc, 2014. [Online]. Available: http://www.merck.com/product/usa/pi_circulars/i/implanon/implanon_pi.pdf. [Accessed 18 Feb 2015].

[109] "Patient Information: Depo-Provera," Pfizer, Inc., 2015. [Online]. Available: http://labeling.pfizer.com/ShowLabeling.aspx?id=522. [Accessed 18 Feb 2015].

[110] W. Mosher and J. Jones, "Use of contraception in the United States: 1982–2008," *National Center for Health Statistics, Vital Health Statistics,* vol. 23, no. 29, 2010.

[111] "How do the pill and other contraceptives work?," The Polycarp Research Institute, 2013. [Online]. Available: http://www.polycarp.org/how_does_the_pill_work.htm. [Accessed 18 Feb 2015].

[112] "Patient Information: Ortho-Micronor," Ortho-McNeil Pharmaceutical, Inc., 2008. [Online]. Available: http://www.accessdata.fda.gov/drugsatfda_docs/label/2008/016954s101lbl.pdf. [Accessed 18 Feb 2015].

[113] B. Pletzer, M. Kronbichler, M. Aichhorn, J. Bergmann, G. Ladurner and H. Kerschbaum, "Menstrual cycle and hormonal contraceptive use modulate human brain structure: Abstract," *Brain Research,* vol. 1348, no. 12, p. 55–62, 2010.

[114] M. Barnes, "Romance and Attraction," 1Flesh.org, [Online]. Available: www.1flesh.org/showcase/contraception-and-romantic-relationships. [Accessed 18 Feb 2015].

[115] D. Scutt and J. Manning, "Ovary and ovulation: Symmetry and ovulation in women," *Human Reproduction,* vol. 11, no. 11, pp. 2477-2480, 1996.

[116] R. Pipitone and G. Gallup, Jr., "Women's voice attractiveness varies across the menstrual cycle: Abstract," *Evolution and Human Behavior,* vol. 29, no. 4, pp. 268-274, 2008.

[117] S. Miller and J. Maner, "Scent of a Woman: Men's Testosterone Responses to Olfactory Ovulation Cues: Abstract," *Psychological Science,* vol. 21, no. 2, pp. 276-286, 2010.

[118] N. Rule, K. Rosen, M. Slepian and N. Ambady, "Mating Interest Improves Women's Accuracy in Judging Male Sexual Orientation: Abstract," *Psychological Science,* vol. 22, no. 7, pp. 881-886, 2011.

[119] K. Cobey, T. Pollet, S. Roberts and A. Buunk, "Hormonal birth control use and relationship jealousy: Evidence for estrogen dosage effects: Abstract," *Personality and Individual Differences,* vol. 50, no. 2, p. 315–317, 2011.

[120] I. Kerner, "Birth control may affect long-term relationships," The Chart, 2012. [Online]. Available: www.thechart.blogs.cnn.com/2012/04/05/birth-control-may-affect-long-term-relationships/. [Accessed 18 Feb 2015].

[121] "Is it OK to use birth control to treat Menorrhagia?," Chastity.com, Catholic Answers Chastity Outreach, [Online]. Available: http://www.chastity.com/question/is-it-ok-to-use-birth-control-to-treat-menorrhagia. [Accessed 18 Feb 2015].

[122] M. Arnold, "Am I right to tell my CCD students they should not take the pill for medical purposes?," Catholic Answers, [Online]. Available: http://www.catholic.com/quickquestions/am-i-right-to-tell-my-ccd-students-they-should-not-take-the-pill-for-medical-purposes. [Accessed 18 Feb 2015].

[123] C. Gnoth, P. Frank-Herrmann, A. Schmoll, E. Godehardt and G. Freundl, "Cycle Characteristics after Discontinuation of Oral Contraceptives," *Gynecological Endocrinology,* vol. 16, no. 4, pp. 307-317, 2002.

[124] L. Candelaria, "Side Effects of Discontinuing Use of a NuvaRing," Livestrong.com, Demand Media, [Online]. Available: http://www.livestrong.com/article/192861-side-effects-of-discontinuing-use-of-a-nuvaring/. [Accessed 18 Feb 2015].

[125] J. Harrison-Hohner, "Getting Pregnant After Depo, Implanon, Ortho Evra Patch and Nuva Ring," The WebMD Health Exchange, 2010. [Online]. Available: http://blogs.webmd.com/womens-health/2010/04/getting-pregnant-after-depo-implanon-ortho-evra-patch-and-nuva-ring.html. [Accessed 18 Feb 2015].

[126] I. Sivin, J. Stern, S. Diaz, M. Pavez, F. Alvarex, V. Brache, D. Mishell, M. Lacarra, T. McCarthy, P. Holma and et al, "Rates and outcomes of planned pregnancy after use of Norplant capsules, Norplant II rods, or levonorgestrel-releasing or copper TCu 380Ag intrauterine contraceptive devices," *American Journal of Obstetrics and Gynecology,* vol. 166, no. 4, 1992.

[127] J. Huber, "Pharmacokinetics of Implanon®. An integrated analysis," *Contraception,* vol. 58, no. 6, pp. 85S-90S, 1998.

[128] A. Glasier, "Implantable contraceptives for women: effectiveness, discontinuation rates, return of fertility, and outcome of pregnancies," *Contraception,* vol. 65, no. 1, pp. 29-37, 2002.

[129] O. Kiriwat, A. Patanayindee, S. Koetsawang, T. Korver and H. Bennink, "A 4-year pilot study on the efficacy and safety of Implanon®. A single-rod hormonal contraceptive implant, in healthy women in Thailand," *The European Journal of Contraception and Reproductive Health Care,* vol. 3, no. 2, pp. 85-91, 1998.

[130] A. Kaunitz, "Beyond the pill: new data and options in hormonal and intrauterine contraception," *American Journal of Obstetrics & Gynecology,* vol. 192, no. 4, pp. 998-1004, 2005.

[131] N. Rue, The Lily Series: The Body Book, Nashville: Tommy Nelson, 2012.

[132] B. Butler, J. Evert and C. Evert, Theology of the Body for Teens: Discovering God's Plan for Love and Life, West Chester: Ascension Press, 2006.

Index

progesterone, 29, 30, 37, 112, 114, 125, 139, 140, 164

protein, 119, 120, 123, 126

puberty, 1, 5, 6, 18, 89, 151

R

rBGH, 125

rBST, 126

rhythm method, 14

S

saturated fats, 122

sleep, 57, 112, 131, 147, 161

soy, 126

sperm, 27, 29, 141

spotting, 9, 47, 48, 113, 144

stress, 3, 59, 95, 97, 98, 99, 100, 101, 131

stroke, 10

T

thermal shift, 68, 69, 70, 71, 72, 73, 78, 81, 86, 89, 93, 152, 164

Thermal Shift Line, 71, 72, 78, 82, 83, 84, 164

thyroid, 104, 108, 126, 162, 164

trans fats, 122, 123

U

underweight, 9, 99, 100

uterus, 7, 26, 27, 28, 29, 30, 89, 106, 116, 140, 141, 151, 161, 162, 163, 164

V

vagina, 26, 48, 49, 51, 53, 113, 139, 161, 162, 164

vaginal infections, 104

vegetables, 119, 123, 125

vegetarian, 100, 120

Vitamin B6, 128

Vitamin E, 127

vitamins, 119, 120, 122, 123, 124, 127

vulva, 26, 29, 59, 164

W

water, 99, 123, 127, 130, 133

wet/stretchy, 54, 65, 66, 67, 78, 86, 90, 93, 98, 102, 152, 158

whole grain, 119

withdrawal bleeding, 141, 164

womb, 26, 35, 141, 164

Y

yeast infections, 104

yoga, 116, 117

   Cat & Cow, 116

   Child's Pose, 116

About the Author

Alison Protz is a Catholic wife, mother of four children, and engineer in Huntsville, Alabama. When she first learned how to understand and chart her own natural cycles, Alison was amazed by the newfound knowledge and wondered why she had not learned this information as a teenager! Talking to many women who share the same sentiment inspired Alison to impart this knowledge in an accessible manner suitable for unmarried chaste teen girls and young women. Raising three daughters, with a commitment to teaching them cycle awareness by God's design, compelled Alison to write *Cycles & Spirituality* so her girls could learn how to understand, appreciate, and live in the modern world with the natural cycles God gave them.

Alison Protz earned a Bachelor of Science degree in Chemical Engineering with a minor in Chemistry from the Massachusetts Institute of Technology (MIT). During her career, she has worked for a major consumer products corporation formulating surfactant and cosmetic products and in the aerospace field leading a team to research, analyze, and solve technical issues with materials and processes pertinent to the nation's space transportation goals. Alison is a technical-minded person who enjoys learning how and why things work. She is co-author on patents and has received peer awards for her ability to communicate technical ideas in a way that helps others understand and implement them.

Alison and her husband, Chris, are a certified Teaching Couple of Natural Family Planning (NFP) with the Couple to Couple League (CCL) and enjoy volunteering their time to teach married and engaged couples how to interpret the signs God gave them to help plan their family. Alison hopes that *Cycles & Spirituality* will introduce girls to cycle awareness at a younger age and enable them to have a better understanding of their own bodies physically, emotionally, and spiritually.